Unbreakable SAINTS

Conquering Life Challenges with a Resilient Spirit

Glenn E. Richardson, PhD

CFI
An Imprint of Cedar Fort, Inc.
Springville, Utah

ISBN 13: 978-1-4621-2048-2

Published by CFI, an imprint of Cedar Fort, Inc.
2373 W. 700 S., Springville, UT 84663
Distributed by Cedar Fort, Inc., www.cedarfort.com

LIBRARY OF CONGRESS CATALOGING-IN-PUBLICATION DATA

Names: Richardson, Glenn E., author.
Title: Unbreakable saints : conquering life challenges with a resilient spirit / by Glenn E. Richardson.
Description: Springville : Cedar Fort, Inc., [2017]
Identifiers: LCCN 2017015876 | ISBN 9781462120482 (pbk. : alk. paper)
Subjects: LCSH: Spiritual life--Church of Jesus Christ of Latter-day Saints. | Mormons--Conduct of life. | Christian life--Mormon authors. | Plan of salvation (Mormon theology)
Classification: LCC BX8656 .R537 2017 | DDC 248.4/89332--dc23
LC record available at https://lccn.loc.gov/2017015876

Cover design by Shawnda T. Craig

Edited and typeset by Kaitlin Barwick

Printed in the United States of America

10 9 8 7 6 5 4 3 2 1

Printed on acid-free paper

To my precious wife, Kathryn, for her patience with my crazy ideas and who read through these chapters to help me transition from university speak to LDS speak.

To my loving parents, Ruth and Glenwood, who had the courage to join the Church and become LDS exemplars so I could be raised with gospel ideals.

To my children who are great examples of resilient living and keep me laughing, smiling, and feeling loved.

To my academic/LDS friends Mark, Camille, Brad, Ken, and Phil who were willing to review this book and provide warming comments.

Praise for
Unbreakable Saints

About twenty years ago, I sat in Dr. Richardson's class as he taught me about being an educator. He uses those excellent teaching skills, his many years of study on resiliency, and his strong testimony and understanding of the Atonement to put together a resource and guide on how to let the Savior's love effect our lives. His storytelling makes the book fun to read. His ideas and activities allow for applying resiliency in our lives. Now I just have to go practice what he preaches.

—Ken Johnson, PhD, associate dean at Weber State University

Dr. Richardson's book provides a unique approach to the plan of salvation by incorporating its principles with the academic literature of resiliency. He lifts the spirit by helping us understand that we are "housing magnificence"; that as we activate our childlike attributes, we can find our special "dirt pile" and make whatever we are doing exciting and fulfilling. We learn how to take life's disruptions and turn them into learning experiences that lead us to mortal and eternal progression. We learn the importance of knowing "which wolf to feed." Life can, and should be fun, and *Unbreakable Saints* helps us understand how to make that possibility a reality. Although our physical and mental progression deteriorates with age, Dr. Richardson helps us see how our spiritual progression can become stronger throughout our mortal sojourn. This is truly a gratifying read and a must read for any individual who wishes to become an Unbreakable Saint.

—J. Mark Jesperson, MBA, former director of temporal affairs

The term "triple threat" is used in theater circles to describe a performer who dazzles in singing, dancing, and acting. When it comes to resiliency, Dr. Glenn Richardson is a bonafide triple threat. He is a leading behavioral and social scientist and scholar in the field of resiliency research; his personal life reflects a successful resilient journey, which allows him to speak from experience with an intimate voice; and he is grounded both spiritually and intellectually as a Latter-day Saint and is uniquely qualified to write about resiliency from a gospel perspective that is both doctrinally credible and personally inspiring.

Unbreakable Saints is a must read for those who seek to understand and appreciate the roles adversity and personal disruption play in a loving God's plan to help us grow and develop. More importantly, this book provides a road map with insights and strategies to apply resilient reintegration on the path to spiritual wholeness.

—Brad Neiger, PhD, associate academic vice president at Brigham Young University

Unbreakable Saints is an inspired discourse on the plan of salvation. Applying the principles of the resiliency theory will awaken your self-worth, aid in your eternal progression, and draw you closer to the Savior.

—Camille Thomas, PhD, professor at Southern Utah University

Contents

An Introduction and Orientation

An appropriate introduction to *Unbreakable Saints* comes from the famous nineteenth-century English novelist Charles Dickens as he began his timeless classic *A Tale of Two Cities*.

> It was the best of times, it was the worst of times, it was the age of wisdom, it was the age of foolishness, it was the epoch of belief, it was the epoch of incredulity, it was the season of Light, it was the season of Darkness, it was the spring of hope, it was the winter of despair, we had everything before us, we had nothing before us, we were all going direct to heaven, we were all going direct the other way. . . .[1]

Unbreakable Saints is a book about encountering the best of times and the worst of times, or more accurately, it is about making the worst of times become the best of times. We know about people who have suffered difficult hardships but because of their spirit, grit, and persistence have thrived in the wake of their adversity. We have read about the ordeals suffered by the Mormon pioneers as they were forced out of their Nauvoo homes, compelled to endure indescribable trials on their journey to resettle into the Salt Lake Valley. We have heard of horrific stories of spousal and child abuse, yet witnessed the survivors surface stronger and wiser. We have seen veterans of foreign wars return home without limbs yet rise to make major contributions to the Church and society. Too many members of the Church have been lured away into the depression and hopelessness of addictions—from drugs to pornography—but those with resilient spirits are able to not only recover but become spiritually stronger.

These are the dramatic stories, but members of the Church are daily faced with challenges, disruptions, demands, and temptations that potentially dampen their spirits. We are exposed to media and social media that attempt to challenge gospel principles and the reputations of our Church leaders. We are in the midst of the "age of wisdom and the age of foolishness." We find ourselves losing our tempers and our patience. We find ourselves gossiping about our brothers and sisters.

Unfortunately, it is too easy to focus on our problems and the problems of others. We spend too little time focusing on our strengths, gifts, and talents that, if nurtured, would see most of our minor problems fade into insignificance. This book is about building your strengths. It is about understanding the psycho-spiritual journey that those who thrive in the face of adversity take in order to turn life challenges into positive experiences. As we seek to understand this mentality, we begin by understanding the journey that is in essence a mini plan of salvation—a process known as *resiliency.*

Resiliency is not only the process and experience of being forced off your ideal spiritual path by temptations, life events, and bad choices but after experiencing a range of emotions and using resiliency and spiritual skills, growing through those challenges to become stronger and more unbreakable. It is a journey we go through regularly. Resiliency is characterized by the energy and motivation to persist in recovering. It is the force or spirit within each of us that motivates us to thrive in the face of adversity.

The resilient spirit is one that recognizes the strength of its childlike nature and applies it to life challenges. It is being able to recognize and access the nobility that has been hidden behind the veil that was put in our minds at birth. It is understanding that we are walking, living, and breathing in a sea of wisdom, courage, and hope that resides within us and within the world around us. We will learn to access that amazing force, whether you label it God's Spirit or whether you want to justify it from an academic perspective using theoretical physics, Eastern healing practices, or Jungian psychology.

As an introduction to *Unbreakable Saints*, let me attempt to unveil the richness of the subtitle that will reveal the essence of how we can encounter and thrive through the "season of Darkness" and experience the "season of Light." Unbreakable by no means suggests that we don't have moments of darkness, discouragement, and despair. The pioneers, the abused, the veterans, and you have all gone through such times. Saints may bend physically, emotionally, and mentally, but the resilient spirit keeps them unbreakable.

The subtitle "Conquering Life Challenges with a Resilient Spirit" poses two powerful concepts. The first word, *conquering*, has multiple meanings that apply directly to our lives. It means to "overcome" and "take control." With all the problems and challenges we face, overcoming and taking control sounds like a breath of fresh air. It also means to "climb successfully."

Successfully climbing over our problems and challenges suggests that we learn and practice intellectual and spiritual skills to become stronger and wiser. *Conquer* also means to gain the love, admiration, and respect of those we serve in our families, at church, and in society. This book is about conquering.

The second part of the subtitle is "Resilient Spirit." Too often in the Church we speak of our own spirits in general terms, and we don't speak enough of the driving forces or yearnings of our own eternal spirit. The powerful light, truth, and wisdom that is housed within our souls is often generalized, and it becomes difficult to discern the specific nature of the spiritual directives we are receiving.

The chapters in this book will first describe the resilient journey we all experience to receive answers to life's disruptions. The resiliency process or mini plan of salvation will describe the stages which are best for receiving answers to life challenges. Subsequent chapters will focus on the nature of your human spirit. You have within you at this time all of the resilient drives and yearnings that you need to become a resilient saint as will be confirmed with scriptures. You will have the opportunity to practice some skills to help access those spiritual yearnings and drives. You will be guided as to how to receive answers from the Spirit, ranging from resonating to quickening. We will talk of what to do with quickening answers and how you develop the skills of self-mastery and the grit and persistence you need to become stronger through each life challenge. This is the essence of the progression of the resilient spirit.

I hope that by the end of this book you will have a treasury of insights and skills to help you deal with life challenges. You will recognize that bending is good to allow for progression and to be in a state to receive personal inspiration with insights. You will also learn how to develop self-mastery in the wake of bending to become more unbreakable.

NOTE

1. Charles Dickens, *A Tale of Two Cities* (London: Chapman & Hall, 1859), 1.

1

The Resilient Journey through the Plan of Salvation

Everyone has a story. In fact, everyone has lots of stories. We recount these life events to family and friends, creating an archive of many treasured memories. Our stories describe adventures, and they also describe challenges. The interesting stories often describe breaks in routine or what we can call disruptions in a normal day. Disruptions can make funny stories or sad stories. The stories last for only a few minutes or for years. They can be planned or unplanned. You may sense the anticipation and excitement of a new story as you plan an adventure. Your story may begin by being blindsided by problems that others create for you. Every story includes agency—the choice to learn and grow from the experience or to not learn from it. Your story is about progressing through mortality. It is about conquering each life experience, whether you venture into it or are blindsided by events.

No matter the story, each experience follows a predictable and controllable journey of potential growth and progression. Understanding the details of the journey and mapping outcomes is the essence of the stories that are told by resilient saints. Every time resilient saints are in chaos or challenging situations, they are stretched and bend but do not break—they bounce back fortified with increased wisdom, strength, and spirit. This chapter will highlight the stages of resiliency as seen in the academic world but enriched with solid gospel principles. The conclusion of this chapter will guide you through resiliency mapping that will help you exercise agency in being able to thrive and progress through life challenges. What is most comforting is that resiliency in the academic literature is founded upon our understanding of the plan of salvation.

Understanding the Plan of Salvation

Years ago when I served as a missionary in Brazil, I and my companions taught six standard missionary discussions. One of the discussions was about the plan of salvation, where we often left investigators in awe as they received answers to the age-old questions "Where did I come from?" "Why am I here?" and "Where am I going?" We spoke of the pre-earth life, where we were warmed by the glory that came from being in the presence of our Father in Heaven. We talked about progressing in spirit to the point where we could no longer progress without a mortal body. People investigating the Church learned of the agency in the Council in Heaven, where we chose to be born into mortality and be tested. We taught about Satan's devilish designs for the earth. In this pre-earth life, the prospect of taking on physical bodies was met with great anticipation from the spirits assembled there. We taught our investigators that when we were born, we started dependent and confused as our spirits took on a body to become a soul—body, mind, and spirit. Early in life, the infant spirit was buried in learning to deal with the demands of the body. The infant soul had to progress by first learning the basics of caring for physical needs, learning skills of the mind, and over time, getting to know the spirit that lived in the pre-earth life with Father in Heaven. We taught that the purpose of our life was to go through the disruptions of mortality, exercise our agency in mastering the passions of our physical bodies, and progress to the point where we could become exalted in celestial glory. When we made mistakes, we could repent and through the Atonement of Christ, receive glory that was lost in the transgression.

> For behold, this is my work and my glory—to bring to pass the immortality and eternal life of man. (Moses 1:39)

If we did not master physical passions, we would find ourselves in a terrestrial or telestial world of glory.

In reviewing these eternal truths, it becomes clear that the plan of salvation provides a grand pattern of eternal progression that simplistically describes our journey from pre-earth life, being disrupted into mortality, and after a trial of our faith, experiencing death. We then will be resurrected into a degree of glory depending upon how much glory we have garnered in this life. Inherent in the plan of salvation are guidelines and concepts that can be used in our daily lives as we strive to progress. The disruptive and recovery pattern essential in the plan of salvation is described in academic literature as "The Metatheory of Resilience and Resiliency."[1]

The Resiliency Connection

Resiliency, like the plan of salvation, follows a pattern that begins in a state of comfort. Inevitably, life problems and challenges happen either by choice or when blindsided by life events. In academic literature, the resilient journey describes the feelings in the aftermath of disruptions as loss, confusion, despair, and hurt. These primary feelings lead resilient people to practice mental, physical, and spiritual skills that lead people to moments of inspiration. With insights to know what to do, resilient saints discover grit and persistence to grow and become stronger through life challenges.

In the scriptures and Church history, we see hundreds of stories from our heroes who have followed the resiliency pattern of disruption and recovery with strength, joy, and increased faith. In 1 Nephi we learn about the disruption of Lehi. The story began in a comfort zone, describing Lehi as a man of means and influence in Jerusalem. Lehi's disruption was triggered by a vision and spiritual promptings. He ventured into the unknown, leaving all of his worldly possessions. He and his family spent years in the trough of difficulty and confusion. With Liahonic guidance, hard work, and a willingness to press forward, they finally found joy when they arrived in a land of bounteous natural resources and were able to rejoice in their freedom. They resiliently recovered.

Enoch was called to preach to the people but did not have the verbal skills to touch lives as the nature of his call required as we can see in his reply to the Lord in Moses 6:31.

> Why is it that I have found favor in thy sight, and am but a lad, and all the people hate me; for I am slow of speech; wherefore am I thy servant?

Yet later in Moses 7:13 we read how, after being in the disruption of self-doubt, feelings of inadequacy, and being overwhelmed by the calling, the Lord blessed Enoch. Enoch recovered with power and confidence.

> So great was the faith of Enoch that he led the people of God, and their enemies came to battle against them; and he spoke the word of the Lord, and the earth

> trembled, and the mountains fled, even according to his command; and the rivers of water were turned out of their course; and the roar of the lions was heard out of the wilderness; and all nations feared greatly, so powerful was the word of Enoch, and so great was the power of the language which God had given him.

We see the same pattern in all the stories in scripture and in daily life. Adam and Eve were living in a state of comfort in the Garden of Eden. They experienced the disruption of eating the forbidden fruit, which changed their living conditions. Ultimately, they were able to find joy in their posterity through the sweat of their brow. The stories continue throughout the scriptures, even as we follow the life of the Savior, who left the pre-earth Council in Heaven as the Firstborn and experienced the disruption of mortal life. He mastered His mortal passions, taught the people, and performed miracles. The Savior experienced the greatest disruptions when suffering beyond understanding in Gethsemane and on the cross. Three days after His death, He was resurrected in glory upon completion of His mortal mission. We see the same journey for the Mormon pioneers who were persecuted and forced to leave their comfort zone in Nauvoo. These pioneers experienced persecution and faced the hardships of crossing the plains and settling into an undesirable desert. With persistence, grit, and self-mastery, the Saints found freedom and prosperity in Utah.

Heroes become heroes because of the way they respond in the face of stressors and disruptions. If they respond with character, faith, vision, and persistence, they master change, challenge, and adversity. In later chapters, you will learn resiliency skills that will help you embrace adversity and adapt them to you help you write your own celestial story.

THE RESILIENT JOURNEY

Resiliency, by definition in academic literature, is the process and experience of being disrupted by life events, adversity, or challenges and in the humbling trough of introspective enlightenment, accessing innate self-mastering strengths to grow stronger through the disruption.[2] To progress, we need to experience the humbling trough of enlightenment before we can grow stronger. As per the stories above, the resilient journey begins at any point in time in a state of homeostasis, shown as step 1 in the resiliency pattern or model.

1: PRE-EARTH LIFE OR HOMEOSTASIS (COMFORT ZONE)

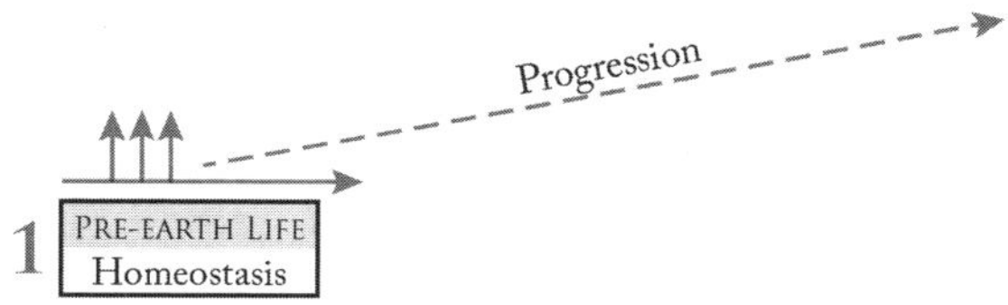

Notice first the long, gradually ascending arrow that represents eternal progression. Although the arrow is straight, suggesting that we harvest glory constantly throughout our lifetimes, the reality is that we gain light, truth, and glory through disruptions and challenges (downs and ups). Progression is the assimilation of glory through life experiences.

Below the line of progression, we see the first stage of the resiliency process: homeostasis, or the pre-earth life if we are thinking about the plan of salvation. We know that we progressed in the spirit world as described in Doctrine and Covenants 138:56.

> Even before they were born, they, with many others, received their first lessons in the world of spirits and were prepared to come forth in the due time of the Lord to labor in his vineyard for the salvation of the souls of men.

Looking at the model, you can see that the solid arrow of this first stage is stagnant, not following the line of progression. In our spiritual life before our earthly journey as we basked in the glory of the Father, we had reached a state where progression was thwarted. We were stagnant and needed to leave the warmth and joy of God's Spirit and take on the challenge of mortality "in the due time of the Lord" (D&C 138:56). Although residing in the glory of our Father in Heaven must have been wonderful, still we probably did not appreciate it because we had yet to experience good and evil, pleasure and pain, or in the resiliency language, disruptions and reintegration. We were foreordained to become gods and goddesses, but we could not progress to that point without becoming a soul—body, mind, and spirit. We needed bodies.

Similarly, in the beginning of the resiliency journey, homeostasis is a state of comfort with no real progression. But unlike the plan of salvation, this point of homeostasis within the resiliency process is temporary and can occur on a daily basis and start at any point in time. You have already experienced the resilient journey thousands of times throughout your life.

To be able to understand the resiliency model, consider a starting point for the journey. It could be now, this point in time while you are reading this book. It is a comfort zone, suggesting that you have adapted to your life situation. Because the resilient journey applies to the different roles and dimensions of your life, you could carry this a step further and specify homeostasis as ecological homeostasis, meaning you have adapted to your living conditions and the people around you. You could also call it biological resilience, suggesting that you have adapted to your state of physical health. You have adapted to your age, your gender, how you look, and how you feel. You could also call it psychological homeostasis, as you have learned many facts and how to do many things in life. You know what you know. You have learned to perform skills and functions to get through a day. Spiritual homeostasis suggests that you have adapted to how close you feel to your Heavenly Father in your life and prayers.

Within this first stage of the model we are building, you will see three upward arrows. These arrows represent your learned protective skills that you have acquired from coping with and growing from previous life challenges. With the disruptions and stressors in your life, you have learned to cope with them and acquired spiritual gifts and strengths from those experiences. In mortality, we have learned lessons on nurturing our bodies. We know how to eat well, exercise, and get adequate sleep. We have learned skills from schools to read, write, plan, and work hard. We have also learned how to be prompted by the spirit to believe gospel principles and be guided in life's choices. Each arrow represents a body, mind, or spirit skill that we have learned and are using to thrive. In reality, there are hundreds of arrows but for simplicity, we show three.

Several years ago, I went through a notable and difficult experience that, for me, exemplified this resiliency process. My homeostasis in this example began as follows:

> It was December 21, the day after my forty-first birthday, and I was exhausted. After my family birthday party, I left the house and drove to the university. I had to finish writing the final chapter for a personal health textbook. The final chapter, entitled "Death and Dying," not only described how I was feeling but perhaps served as an omen and warning of things to come. Following my all-nighter, I had a meeting with some faculty members at the School of Nursing to make final revisions for a grant proposal that was due by the end of the year. I yearned to go home. Students were gone for the holidays, turning the campus into a virtual ghost town. I was finally going to be away from the hassles of work and be with my wife and

four children for Christmas. As I walked down the hill toward my car, I breathed deeply as the invigorating winter air filled my lungs. Even with my sleepless fatigue, I felt a great sense of accomplishment and peace.

2: Need to Progress and Life Events

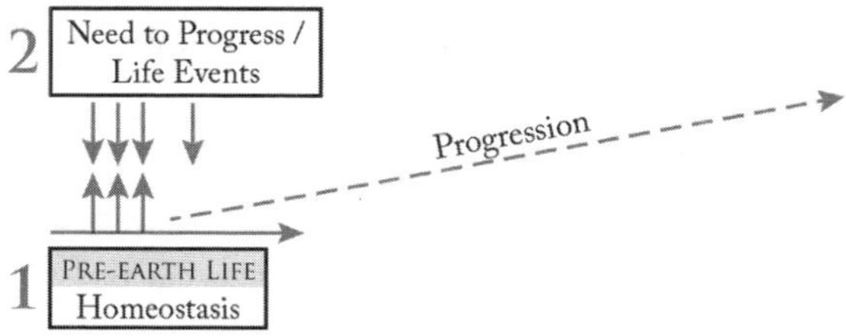

Box 2 represents those life events that potentially affect our homeostasis. Sometimes we choose to take on new opportunities for growth, and at other times, we are blindsided by unexpected events and need to learn coping skills. In our resiliency model, the upward arrows represent skills we have previously learned, while the downward arrows represent new challenges, stressors, or experiences that threaten our homeostasis.

In the pre-earth life, our spirits longed to become souls and experience mortality and to prove ourselves. We needed to take on the challenge of mortality.

> And we will prove them herewith, to see if they will do all things whatsoever the Lord their God shall command them;
>
> And they who keep their first estate shall be added upon; and they who keep not their first estate shall not have glory in the same kingdom with those who keep their first estate; and they who keep their second estate shall have glory added upon their heads for ever and ever. (Abraham 3:25–26)

You can reflect upon your own life and see that you have several learned skills that help you negotiate through life's challenges. You can problem solve, read, prepare a meal, earn a living, and use numerous other skills that help you deal with life challenges. For new experiences, such as coming to earth, we have no experience or protective arrows. The need to progress helped us to take the leap of faith to earth and believe that we will be able to harvest enough glory to return to our Father in Heaven.

In order to progress in the plan of salvation, our spirits needed to take on a physical body and become a soul. The fourth arrow that comes down from box 2 in the model represents new life experiences. These are events or challenges that we have not experienced before. People investigating the Church encounter new principles when missionaries teach discussions. In the rapidly changing world of technology, we all find ourselves faced with new arrows regularly as we face the challenge of learning how to use new electronic devices.

3: Birth and Venturing

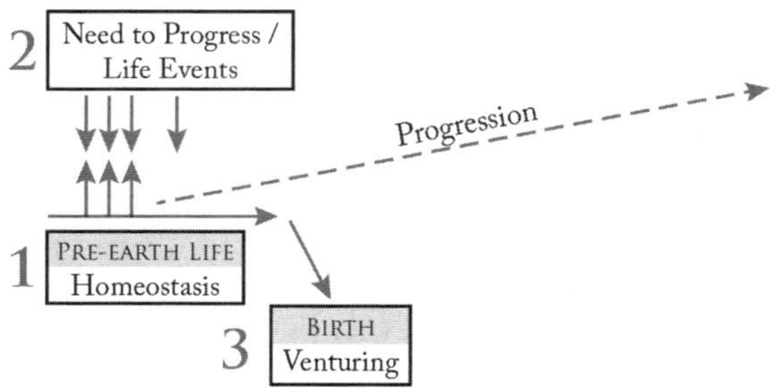

Box 3 represents the leap of faith from the pre-earth life in glory in an experience we call birth. During birth our spirits enter the physical body in a strange new world. It takes some time to develop the listening skills to let the Spirit guide in the shadow of noisy physical and mental demands for survival. In our beginning days of mortality, our physical needs scream louder than the soft gentle promptings of the spirit. Onlookers can see the spirit in a baby as he or she radiates goodness and innocence, but the immature mind and body of the infant are essentially helpless. We are born with innate physical needs and drives to eat, sleep, and be active. We are in new situation, and our conscious minds have no recollection of the glorious life with the Father. We are disoriented and confused, not knowing how to walk or eat or even communicate except with crying. We are totally dependent upon a nurturer to take care of us.

The resilient journey is similar except that we can remember our previous states of homeostasis. Venturing is leaving homeostasis and encountering new life events, stressors, and other changes that propel us into disruptions. The life events may or may not be in our control. Sometimes we are blindsided by the actions of others, by electronics that suddenly don't work, or even the weather. Sometimes we are disrupted by yielding to temptation and committing sins that disrupt us into guilt.

Optimally, resiliency is much like birth in that we take a leap of faith into new adventures to learn, grow, and progress. You go to school, get a job, have children, and learn new skills, which are potentially positive but still take us away from homeostasis. Even studying the gospel and striving to live a more Christlike life requires changes in thought and actions but still takes us away from homeostasis and allows us to grow beyond our previous state. Venturing, when you are blindsided, can result in major disruption, but remember that these experiences are the essence of progression. In my own story, the venturing via being blindsided began as I started to cross the street:

> I approached the road that divided the upper campus from the traditional academia of main campus. At the crosswalk, a van had stopped to let me cross the first of four lanes. From this moment until thirteen days later, I have little conscious recall of the events that ensued. I will continue this story based upon the reports from the physicians, police, and paramedics.

> As I stepped past the van into the second of four lanes, a 1982 Oldsmobile came barreling down the road at 45 miles per hour (in a 30 mph speed zone). The driver—a foreign student who had only lived in the states for a few weeks and had just received a license to drive—did not even slow down. The Olds's bumper struck my lower legs, shattering the bones into small pieces. My body flipped up onto the hood of the passenger side of the car. Since I was lifted onto the side of the hood, the impact caused me to spin. My head struck the passenger side window and shattered it. The Olds drove on for several hundred yards before the terrified foreign student realized what had happened. I lay in an unconscious heap on the side of the road. Fortunately, the first car to stop was a physician who worked at the nearby University Hospital. He jumped out of the car and held me in his arms. There was little doubt in his mind that I would die. A hundred yards from the crosswalk, as fortune would have it, was a fire station staffed with paramedics. In a short time, I was put into an ambulance and hurried to the hospital that I had left only minutes before with feelings of relief. Now I was returning comatose in an ambulance, precariously close to death.

All stories require an event, new information, or change to really be a story. Life events take us from our homeostasis. Some events are like the experience in the story—getting hit by a car. Maybe not life-threatening but unsettling are other major life events such as divorce, financial crises, and family conflicts. Other events are minor, such as friends and family making us change plans, running out of gas, or forgetting an item at the store. Desired and optimal changes are leaps of faith into new learning experiences such as taking a class, reading a book, or looking for a new job. All of our stories begin with homeostasis. We venture into disruptions prompted by a life event or change or choice. The change begins a new story of our lives.

4: Primary Emotions and Skills

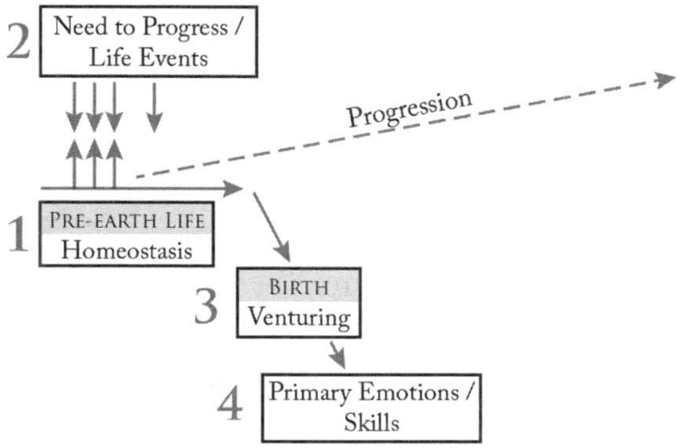

Box 4 describes the feelings following disruptions. The primary emotions of hurt, loss, guilt, and fear are common after we take the leap of faith into new adventures. We feel these emotions with most new events. We have some fear about taking a class. We may sense that we are wasting some time by going on vacation. We are anxious about starting an exercise program or learning a new skill. These positive ventures may be accompanied by fear of failure. Being blindsided by events are also accompanied with hurt feelings, loss of control, guilt for not being better prepared, and again, the fear of the outcomes.

Both anticipated venturing as well as forced venturing propel us into disruptions. The important primary outcome of a disruption is humility and openness to receive help from God to get us through the experience and, after recovery, celebrating the infusion of Spirit. In the state of humility, we often find ourselves on our knees seeking help and guidance. Prayer is the essential skill to receive answers. In resiliency training, prayer, along with meditation, imagery, music, art therapy, and dozens of other skills, are taught to help us prepare to receive answers, courage, and strength to work through the resilient journey.

The first emergency-room physician did not think to check for internal bleeding, but as I ballooned in size, the astute supporting nurse practitioner realized I was in trouble. I was bleeding to death. They had to cut off my wedding ring because my fingers were swelling rapidly and the ring was cutting off the circulation. They performed a fasciotomy (an eight-inch surgical slit) on both of my legs to release some of the fluid pressure that was bloating me.

I was rolled into surgery on repeated occasions. The first surgery was to remove my ruptured and bleeding spleen. Another surgery was to put rods down my legs and slide the broken bones around the rods so the bones could heal. The surgeon described it as making macaroni necklaces on a string, like we created back in elementary school. They put four round six-and-a-half-inch screws into each of my lower legs for support and left four inches of the screws protruding from my legs. They left my fractured hip to heal without any clinical intervention. They monitored my head trauma regularly. I would be in a coma through Christmas and New Year's Day.

My first recollection was one of discomfort. My head hurt. I was confused and disoriented. What had happened? I opened my eyes to see my wife whom I recognized. She asked me, "Do you know where you are?"

As I looked around in my intensive-care hospital room with the many tubes in my body and machines all around me, I responded matter-of-factly with an academic tone, "It appears to be some sort of clinical setting." I immediately went back to sleep after my analytical response. I was not awake enough to begin to understand what was happening to me.

The next day I woke again, and my wife was there, shaving my face with an electric razor. This time I could feel the right side of my brain starting to work again. I have always enjoyed a good laugh and joking around. I saw the razor, took it from my wife, and began to use it as a microphone as I started singing "Tutti Frutti, Oh Rudy." Again, I slipped back to sleep. I imagine my wife and the medical staff wondered at that point if the brain trauma was permanent.

As I slowly emerged from my coma, I was awake for longer periods and became conversational with visitors. As the reality of the accident started to sink into my mind, I began to wonder what I was going to do. I first felt bad for my wife and children who were worrying about their husband and father who was in a coma and precariously close to death. I ached for them. I thought about how my poor mother might be feeling with her tender emotions still evident as a relatively new widow. I wondered about my work. I was a department chair at the university and knew faculty and staff would be affected. Following visits from family, colleagues, and friends, I realized that my loved ones would be OK, but I felt bad for the emotional distress they were going through.

I laid in the hospital for another week. It was a time of wondering, pondering, introspection, and remembering. With my strong belief that Heavenly Father loved me, I found myself repeatedly in a state of prayer and meditation. I knew my fate was in the hands of some of the greatest medical professionals in the world, but more than that, I felt that I needed the help of a power well beyond the skills of even the greatest physicians. I was in the process of learning that these kinds of massive events, which seem to be beyond human control, come from a collective destiny designed to redirect my life path.

I found myself questioning my future during the long, dark, and painful nights. As I looked at the four pins sticking out of each of my lower legs,

> I questioned, "Will I ever walk again? What am I to do? What am I to be? Will I ever be able to teach again?" I had always been an optimist of sorts and assumed that I would fully recover—but would I? I needed guidance, comfort, and peace to know what to do and to give me strength to recover from this accident.

5: Inspiration / Resonation and Quickening

Box 5 on the resiliency or plan of salvation model is inspiration or personal revelation, which is in the trough of disruption. In mortality, resonation and quickening of the spirit is the most desirable feast that we can enjoy in mortality. To be connected to the sea of God's glory in which we live brings all the qualities we really want in life. We want understanding, peace, love, guidance, comfort, hope, and all the other qualities the Spirit brings. We have been promised that we can receive the things that we seek.

> For he that diligently seeketh shall find; and the mysteries of God shall be unfolded unto them, by the power of the Holy Ghost, as well in these times as in times of old, and as well in times of old as in times to come; wherefore, the course of the Lord is one eternal round. (1 Nephi 10:19)

We can see in box 5 the trough of inspiration, resonation, and quickening.

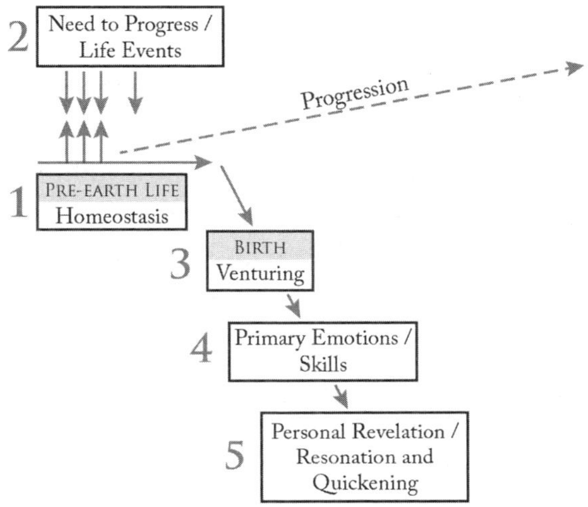

Optimally, humility and openness are the products of disruptions. Step 5 in the resilient journey or plan of salvation process is the quest for knowing what to do and how to deal with life challenges. We receive the answers through personal revelations or inspiration. The scriptures talk about the spirit resonating and quickening our souls to know truth. In Doctrine and Covenants 88:17–18 and 49, we read the following passages that speak of being quickened by the Spirit:

> And the redemption of the soul is through him that quickeneth all things, in whose bosom it is decreed that the poor and the meek of the earth shall inherit it.
>
> Therefore, it must needs be sanctified from all unrighteousness, that it may be prepared for the celestial glory. . . .
>
> The light shineth in darkness, and the darkness comprehendeth it not; nevertheless, the day shall come when you shall comprehend even God, being quickened in him and by him.

In future chapters, we will discuss how to be quickened. Interestingly, in the resiliency literature, we call the experience of receiving answers to life challenges *resonation* and *quickening.* In a state of humble readiness, you can receive insights to know what to do, when to do it, and have the energy to make it happen. These defining moments infuse your soul with the qualities you really want in life including peace, hope, courage, direction, and wisdom. Your unbreakable and thriving life is one in which you know that each step of your story is in harmony with what is best for you and is a path of glory acquisition. You have within you an innate script for an optimal life. The gentle reading of your life script (foreordination) is called *resonation.* You will also feel dramatic moments in your story that are very impactful and life changing. Defining moments or life-changing inspirations are the quickening moments. The essence of your amazing life story is to be in harmony with your subtle resonations to truths and answers and to act upon moments of quickening.

With resonation and quickening, your goal is to make the veil between mortality and the spirit world become very thin. In our humble state, we read scriptures, take the sacrament, provide service, and listen to speakers who have discovered the means to share their spiritual nature. We hope to receive spiritual promptings from our Heavenly Father that will guide us through our life challenges.

With regular experiences with the Spirit, we acquire skills and wisdom to help us harvest light, truth, and intelligence to the point that the veil becomes very thin. President Uchtdorf taught, "As we draw near to Heavenly Father, we become more holy. . . . This greater light leads to the unspeakable ministerings of the Holy Spirit, and the veil between heaven and earth can become thin."[3] The veil is thin when there is a free flow of spirit-to-spirit communications that guide our spirits to take control of the soul. We feel the qualities of peace, assurance, confidence, hope, and guidance as we celebrate the progression in the mortal experience as it gradually begins to control the body. More detail on how to resonation and quickening will be provided in chapter 7.

As described earlier in the story, I was experiencing primary emotions as part of stage 4 of the model. I was confused. I hurt all over. I was worried that I would never recover. I didn't know what would happen to me. The next part of the story embraces stage 5, resonation and quickening.

> During my week of pondering while in the hospital, my mind kept going back to my only vivid memory of the time in my coma. I don't know if the memory coincided with Christmas Eve or not, but it did coincide with a time when the doctors indicated that my condition was worsening. About this time, I do remember a precious moment—a moment that even when I ponder it to this day, years later, I still feel stirrings of peace and joy.
>
> As I was starting to slip away from this mortal life, I felt like I was basking in a peaceful warmth. I felt so good. To my right, I became aware of a light. I looked and saw a large opening into what seemed like a beautiful oasis, but the opening was covered with a veil. I could see how luminous it was on the other side, yet it was somewhat opaque and I couldn't really make out what was on the other side. From this lighted veil was an energy and feeling of love and peace that overwhelmed my soul. I felt like I was almost melting under the influence of a loving energy that came from that opening. I bathed myself in this radiant loving light much like I used to do lying on a beach near my hometown of San Diego.
>
> I remember questioning what was beyond the veil. As I pondered what was happening, I suddenly felt two hands from behind me gently slide onto my shoulders. First, the fingers touched the top of my shoulders, then I felt the fingers slide down until the palms of the hands were firmly resting on

me. The hands were strong yet gentle. The hands were filled with such energy and love that when they touched my shoulders, it was like an electric current. I never saw a face, but I knew it was my father who had passed away a couple of years before. His nonverbal message was short, comforting, and penetrating: "Buzz Ole Man, you will live. Stay the course." Dad always called me *Buzz Ole Man*. It sounds funny to write, but when he spoke it, it was endearing.

"Stay the course" was part of the counsel he would give me as a boy when we would go camping or when he would take me on his business trips. It was amazing to me the volume of communication that occurred with so few words.

His message was accompanied by visions of grandeur, direction, and awe. "You will live" was full of personal and family implications filled with hope. "Stay the course" was accompanied with a vision of both a mission in life with regards to my family and community as well as my academic career. I could look at my children and see the light in their eyes and the majesty of their spirits. In my work, I was just beginning to ponder the concept of resiliency and trying to understand how people grow stronger through adversity.

When he said to me "stay the course," there was no question as to what that course was—it was to be my life story. It was clear to me that my journey for the rest of my life would be a life carrying a resilient compass. I knew my purpose was to help people thrive through adversity. I wanted to touch hearts and, more important, have people nurture their own hearts. The range of the vision of "stay the course" was from nurturing my family to touching lives in academia and the community. I have no idea how long the experience lasted, but it was as clear as any experience I had ever had.

> Many people who have these kinds of experiences share them with others, but I did not for many years. Even now, I cannot express the full measure or details of that glorious day.
>
> A few days later, I again woke from my coma, but everything was different. Rather than questioning my future, I was confident. I felt a remarkable relief and freedom from my pain. I felt as though I was a baby again, wrapped in a warm and cuddly blanket. The feelings I had were amazing, comforting, and exciting! I sensed that I was being consumed by love. It was exhilarating, and I felt more cherished than I ever had before. I learned what real happiness was. I knew from this experience that I would recover.

6: SELF-MASTERY/RESURRECTION

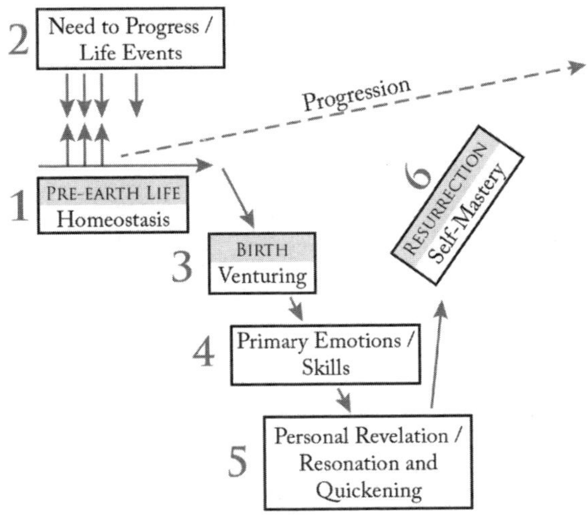

Once we gain insights or the "truth of all things," the resilient journey continues through the stage of self-mastery, stage 6. Self-mastery builds on the concept of quickening and embraces the concepts of faith, grit, and persistence. It also includes the idea of creating a new personal identity that will best deal with the disruptions. To lead the children of Israel out of captivity, Moses changed identities twice. His original identity was that of nobility, living in Pharaoh's court, which changed when he fled the court as a fugitive in the wake of his defending a Hebrew slave. His identity later changed again when God called him as a prophet to lead the children of Israel out of bondage. Housed within each soul is an array of identities that can surface in response to the challenges we face. Guidelines on how to access these identities as part of self-mastery will be addressed in chapter 8. You can be more courageous, more humble, more honest, or whatever identity best negotiates the disruption you are facing. Faith is also a dimension of this self-mastery. The goal of this stage is to harness innate human drives and yearnings to magnify your faith.

Self-mastery is the key to overcoming physical addictions to free yourself from the energy-consuming world of guilt. Power and motivation are the essence of resilience. It is the force that comes from spiritual sources. You will ponder in later chapters how to access that force. My story continues with self-mastery as the focus.

> I woke up and knew that I would recover. I knew I needed to pursue the academic path to discover the depth and richness of resiliency because it was clear to me that this area of academic work was in harmony with gospel ideals. It would be preaching the gospel using different names. My ponderings during the endless hours in the hospital after I awoke from the coma were about how I could help people become stronger in the face of challenging life events. I had received an enlightening moment that let me know what I was to do with my professional life. I realized that I needed to live to be able to tell the story of recovery.
>
> While I woke from the coma with a vision of my future, I also woke up to see the long screws protruding from my legs and realizing that I had lost two weeks of my life. The academic part of me felt guilty

for wasting so much time. I was writing a book and had deadlines. Then the reality of my situation began to sink in and I realized that I had almost lost my life. I then realized what my family had been through for two weeks, not knowing if I would live or die and if I would be the same even if I did survive. The thought broke my heart, and I wept and wept alone in my hospital room. When the kids came up to see me, they were nervous and unsure of how to act. Before the accident, they would run to me and we would wrestle, joke, and play. Now, I didn't look good—I didn't even look like their dad because I had been beaten up so badly by the car. The children were confused and didn't know whether to hug me or not because it might inflict more pain. Several thoughts, emotions, and questions ran through my mind. I struggled to wrap my mind around what had just happened.

After returning home I realized that my rehabilitation journey was really just beginning, now without the nurturing help of the hospital staff. With velcro casts on both legs and pins in my legs, I learned to use my arms to lift myself step by step to reach my bedroom on the second floor of my home. I learned to wash by sitting on the floor of the shower with my legs dangling outside. Still, there were dozens of discouraging moments. I had always been physically active and enjoyed sports, and now I was stuck in a wheelchair. But because of what I had experienced, I knew my path was directed by a strength and power beyond myself.

As weeks passed, I became impatient with my slow healing, in spite of my doctors telling me that I was rehabilitating faster than expected. After much planning, I determined a way to drive my Ford F-250 pickup after a couple of weeks. I felt so free to be able to run errands, even with my legs in casts and the pins still sticking out of my lower legs.

> I had learned that I would live. I knew my mission. I can't remember a time in my life that I was more motivated. I knew that Dad's spirit was close, and I reflected again and again on the loving power of his hands on my shoulder with the words "stay the course" as my mantra. I had read the scriptures, but now they became real. I didn't want to be an administrator any more. I decided to focus my career on teaching and move more deeply into the world of resilience. Nothing would deter me. I was determined to be a rehabilitation warrior! I pushed the limits.

7–9: Resilient Reintegration (Wisdom) and the Degrees of Glory

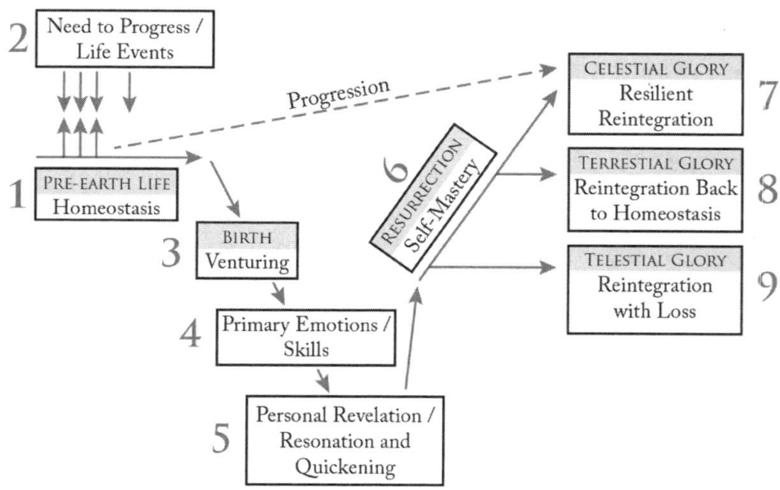

As we look at the plan of salvation, we see that we all go through the same big disruption—gaining a physical body. But degrees of glory we may earn vary based upon the light and truth we are able to garner during our mortal lives. We gather glory by our works.

> And it came to pass that I said unto them that it was a representation of things both temporal and spiritual; for the day should come that they must be judged of

> their works, yea, even the works which were done by the temporal body in their days of probation. (1 Nephi 15:32)

Works is an inclusive term that embraces body, mind, and spirit, which indicates that what we do (body), think (mind), and feel (spirit) are the works that will be judged. If we thrive through life challenges by finding wisdom, accomplishment, serving others, and living with character, then we will harvest enough glory to feel comfortable in the celestial kingdom.

> For after much tribulation come the blessings. Wherefore the day cometh that ye shall be crowned with much glory; the hour is not yet, but is nigh at hand. (D&C 58:4)

From a resiliency perspective, we become wiser with each disruption and resilient reintegration. Each new experience provides an opportunity to learn how we got into the disruption and what the outcome was. As we continue to experience disruption after disruption, over time we increase in wisdom and consequently progression.

We can look at wisdom and progression as a worldview puzzle that begins at birth. As you enter the world, you experience your first disruptions—a physical body. From the womb, you experience the change from the watery and warm comfort of the womb, to the world of air and cold. The first piece of your life puzzle after birth is having to use your lungs to breathe. You meet Mom and Dad (two new pieces). You continue to be bombarded by new pieces of input from the external world and internal world that disrupt and reform your worldview puzzle. More and more pieces of the world are thrown at you. You ride in a car for the first time as you travel home. You are greeted by new family members. You go to school and face the challenges of academics and social interactions. You are also exposed to gospel principles and hopefully have glory-infusing experiences while attending Young Men and Young Women meetings. You feel infusion of glory in seminary, institute, youth conferences, general conference, and testimony meetings.

Each of these new pieces cause your worldview to disrupt, cause change, and may be become chaotic, but then you reintegrate. Resilient reintegration is to add the new experience or piece of the puzzle to your worldview. Your worldview gets bigger and bigger as you learn to negotiate life with new skills and insights. You become wiser and increase in glory because of your experiences. This reintegration is the concluding stage of the resilient journey. The goal here is not only to recover but to become stronger and wiser. Your life puzzle or view of the world becomes grander and more glorious as you increase in wisdom. Negotiating the resilient journey allows you to tell the story of disruption and reintegration. You build your arsenal of stories to personally become unbreakable and to be able to help others know how to access glory and wisdom in their world.

If we moderately live by the principles of the gospel and teachings of the Savior, then we will likely harvest enough glory in the mortal experience to feel comfortable in a terrestrial glory. When speaking of resiliency, we recover or reintegrate but we really do not progress. If we violate the commandments of God, then we will likely radiate enough glory for the telestial kingdom. Telestial reintegration on the resiliency map is shown as reintegration with loss, ending at a point with less motivation, drive, and glory than the original homeostasis.

Resiliency parallels the plan of salvation in recognizing that we have agency. We can choose to resiliently reintegrate and gain wisdom throughout our lifetime. We develop skills and competence as we cope and thrive through life problems and challenges. Resilient saints are those that consciously reintegrate with more thriving skills following disruptions. These are what we might call celestial choices. Some people shy away from life's challenges and choose not to learn from them, returning instead to the stagnation of their comfort zones or making terrestrial choices. Still others become disgruntled by life challenges and become angry and bitter, which seems to be a telestial choice.

Resiliency Mapping with the Plan of Salvation

As you reflect upon the big picture of your life, you may be able to see where you are along the resilient journey. The reality is that you are in different stages for each of the dimensions and roles you have. You may be in the homeostasis stage where everything has become routine in your church calling. Perhaps you are in a disruption with hurt and guilt if you are in the midst of an argument with one of them. You may be comfortable living within a budget, or you may be experiencing a disruption with unexpected bills. You may be comfortable with your worthiness, or you may be disrupted by something that you thought or did that was outside of your moral framework. You may be happy where you live, or you may be feeling the urge to move.

With each dimension of your life, you can reflect upon where you are along your resilient journey, a practice called *resiliency mapping*. This is the process of reflecting upon where you are, planning where you want to be, and being aware of the emotions that you experience along your resilient journey. As you are conscious of the process and active in choosing to reintegrate resiliently, you will find that you have developed new skills or felt increased glory.

The image on page 37 has the boxes representing the stages of the resiliency process. You can reference the previous models to remember the nature of each stage. Reflect upon some dimension of your life. Perhaps it is a prompting from your physical body that you need to exercise or eat better. You can map your journey through the process of assuring that you are physically capable of doing exercise (from a physician), then pondering what exercise would be most enjoyable, then venturing to actually exercise. You will be disrupted with the new experience. It will take time away from other activities. It will cause soreness on the front end. But with self-mastery, you will endure. After a few weeks, you will resiliently reintegrate and feel more energy, think clearer, and feel fit.

Resiliency mapping with spiritual challenges follows the same pattern. If, for example, you happen to have a situation at work where coworkers speak disparagingly of the Church, over time you may begin to ponder their negative comments. Doubts could begin to emerge. You decide to sit down and map out this experience.

You can map this by first filling in the homeostasis box 1, describing how you felt before your coworkers' comments. You might put "feeling comfortable with my testimony of the gospel." Box 2 will be filled with the elements of the comments that could cause you to doubt. Box 3 will describe a commitment to resolve your questioning or doubts.

Box 4 may require much more space than you have in the little box. Perhaps you can do some journaling (a skill) to express your feelings of doubt. Maybe you will plan to walk in nature to allow yourself some uninterrupted time to reflect upon the effect the comments had on you. With trusted loved ones, you might express the feelings of your heart about the comments.

In box 5 you will describe how you want to feel the resonation of truth and be quickened again by the Spirit. You will plan to take time to ponder the spiritual confirmations of truth from your past experiences. You will plan to read those key scriptures to which you have always resonated. You will know that before you can fill box 6 on self-mastery, you will need to wait for the quickening moment. In your mapping, you will know that you have to continue to read the scriptures, pray, take meditative walks, and reflect upon past quickening moments.

You will then be able to fill in box 6 on self-mastery and make a plan as to how to resist the influence of faith-doubting coworkers. Perhaps part of your self-mastery is to write an extensive accounting of the journey of doubt followed by a spiritual account of your quickening. You will be able to use this account for future questioning moments.

The remaining three boxes allow you to reflect upon the outcomes, whether you resiliently reintegrate, reintegrate back to homeostasis, or reintegrate with loss. In box 7 you can describe how the experience has built your testimony. You can celebrate the initial doubt because it forced you to work at your testimony and consequently you have harvested a little more glory. In box 8 you return to homeostasis or to the same base-line testimony without an increase in faith or glory. Your testimony remains stagnant. In box 9 your doubts continue, and you find reasons to complain and criticize the Church. You become angry and bitter and consequently leave the Church.

You can map other challenges as well. Perhaps you are trying to overcome a habit that causes you guilt. You can map the journey of recognizing how homeostasis (doing or thinking the undesirable habit) makes you feel guilty and diminishes your sense of self-worth. You can then map your venture to overcome the habit through study and gathering energy from your resilient or spiritual drives (which we will discuss over the remainder of this book). With those drives, you will be able to overcome your undesirable habit.

If you are blindsided by life events, you still go through the process, the difference being how you get into the journey. Rather that you choosing to venture into improving your mental, spiritual, or physical health, you now go through the disruptive trough because of circumstance.

Take the opportunity to try to do some resiliency mapping for any life challenges you have or for any drives you have to improve the health and wellbeing of your body, mind, spirit, or relationships with others. This is a map to harvest glory.

The resiliency process and the plan of salvation is the pathway that all resilient saints follow. It is the pathway to become unbreakable—bendable, but not breakable. Future chapters provide instruction on how to develop skills of the soul that will help you go through the resilient journey resiliently reintegrating and mapping the journey to conquer each new disruption or challenge. You will learn skills to experience resonation and quickening, which gives you the power to bounce back stronger and even more unbreakable in the face of adversity. You will receive guidance as to how to increase your faith and self-mastery. The next chapter will focus on your innate resilience which is how to access energy and motivation to thrive through adversity.

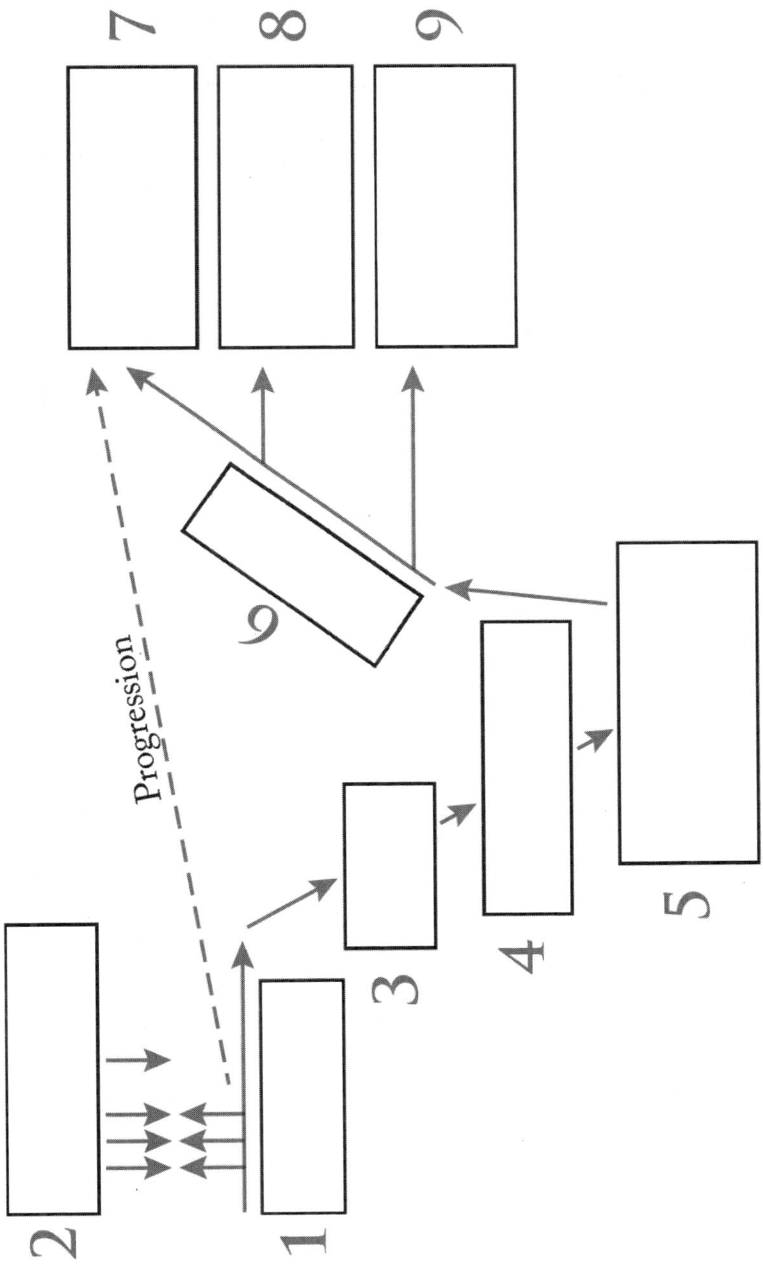
7
8
9
6
5
4
3
Progression
2
1

Notes

1. Glenn E. Richardson, "The Metatheory of Resilience and Resiliency," *Journal of Clinical Psychology* 58, no. 3 (March 2002): 307–21, doi: 10.1002/jclp.10020.
2. See Glenn E. Richardson, *Proactive and Applied Resilience: The Sixteen Experiences* (Bloomington, IN: iUniverse, forthcoming).
3. Dieter F. Uchtdorf, "The Love of God," *Ensign*, November 2009, 23–24.

2

THE UNBREAKABLE RESILIENT SPIRIT

ACCESSING THE GLORY OF YOUR NOBILITY

Now that we have explored the resiliency journey as explained by the plan of salvation, we can now rediscover your innate motivation, drive, and energy to be able to thrive and progress through the unbreakable resilient journey. The motivations from a gospel perspective are clear—they are the yearnings of the Spirit within you. Too often, we only reach out to access guidance and power from the Spirit of God without reflecting upon the amazing power within you and your ability to connect with your experienced spirit. In the next chapter, we will explore the oneness of our spirits with that of the Light of Christ. But for now, we will explore the nature of your unbreakable resilient spirit.

From the academic world, motivation and drive comes from innate resilience. Resilience is a force within everyone that drives him/her to seek self-actualization, altruism, wisdom, and harmony with a source of spiritual strength. Your resilient spirit has the yearning and motivation to acquire light, truth, and guidance from spiritual sources. We will talk of childlike, character, ecological, and universal resilience in future chapters, but this chapter will focus on your noble resilience. Noble resilience is the drive within you to feel valued, important, and have a sense of self-worth.

> Where resiliency is the process of acquiring glory in mortality, resilience is the yearning and force within each person to thrive and acquire glory through the resilient journey. Resilience is the motivation is fulfill your foreordination.

Before we explore the self-motivating driving forces and yearnings of your resilient spirit, let's first review where we are on the resiliency model. From chapter 1, remember that the first stage of the resilient journey is homeostasis or the comfort zone as shown in the figure below. If we put this in the framework of the plan of salvation, the first stage is our first estate or pre-earth life.

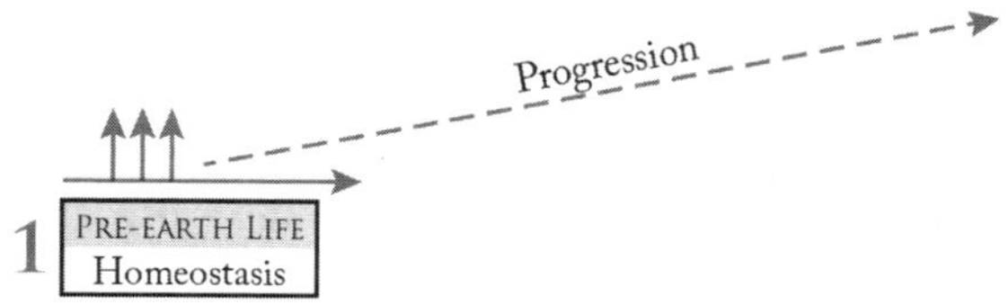

We learned that we can use the resiliency model to map out our plan to grow and progress through life experiences. We know that progression in mortality is the harvesting of glory, light, and truth along the resilient journey. Conquering life challenges through disruption and resilient recovery is the mechanism to become an unbreakable saint. We will first focus on the gifts, strengths, power, and resources you had and still have within you when you harvested glory in the first estate. Secondly, we will take a journey into the reservoirs of your unconscious mind based upon the work by the great

Swiss psychiatrist Carl Gustav Jung, which will give a new meaning to genealogy work as a source of glory. We will use the term "glory" in this book freely as it is referenced in the scriptures as "intelligence, or, in other words, light and truth" (D&C 93:36). The nature of glory will be explained in detail in chapter 4.

GLORY FROM THE FIRST ESTATE

The glory, memories, and experiences your spirit had in the first estate are still within you. The reservoir of light and wisdom housed within the recesses of your soul are beyond earthly comprehension. One of the purposes of mortality is to access the glory that is within you that was inherited from your Father in Heaven as the Father of your spirit.

Housed within your soul is a treasury of gifts, strengths, and talents that are well beyond your normal conscious thinking. The innate motivational forces are called *resilience*. By definition, resilience is a force within everyone that drives him or her to seek self-actualization, altruism, wisdom, peace, and harmony with a source of spiritual strength.

The primary purpose in life is to access the treasury of spiritual diamonds that will help you to thrive and progress through the challenges of life. In times of decision, distress, confusion, and weakness, so many of us quickly look to others or some wisdom from the outside to help us. The truth is that the answers to most of your life questions are housed within you. You have magnificent diamonds of wisdom, spirit, and energy housed within you.

To reinforce the focus for the discovery of your innate resilience energy, let's consider a story by Dr. Russell H. Conwell. Dr. Conwell was a Union officer during the Civil War and later became the founder and president of Temple University. He learned this story from his guide when he traveled through ancient Persia. Here is a paraphrased version of the original story.

> Ali Hafed owned a large farm made up of orchards, grain fields, and gardens. He was well respected in the community and was very wealthy. He had a wonderful family and was leading a life of contentment. One of the wisest men in Ali's community was a Buddhist priest who often visited and provided counsel to the people in the region.
>
> One day the priest came to visit Ali. After passing some time with Ali and his family, telling them how the world was made, the Buddhist priest told Ali in the glimmer of an evening fire that the most precious thing in the entire world was a stone that was a gift from the sun. This stone, called a diamond, contained a drop of sunlight whose glitter would warm any heart. The old priest told Ali that if he had one diamond the size of his thumb, he could purchase the entire community in which he lived. And if he could find a handful of diamonds, he could place his children upon thrones.
>
> The words of the old priest pierced Ali Hafed's heart like a spear. Ali became consumed with the thought of diamonds. He could hardly eat or sleep because of his visions of finding diamonds. In one day, without losing anything, Ali Hafed changed from being a contented and wealthy man to becoming a discontented and poor man. He had lost nothing but had heard of this wonderful stone called a diamond. Now he wanted diamonds more than anything in the world.
>
> He asked all over about where he could find diamonds. Neither the Buddhist priest nor anyone in the community knew. The priest said that somewhere in the world there is a place with plenty of diamonds. Ali Hafed made up his mind; he had to go and find

them. He sold his beautiful farm and left his family in the care and keeping of family members. He left much of his money with his family but took what he thought would be enough money with him to fund his journey. He purchased camels, packed them with food and supplies, and hired several servants to accompany him on his quest. Ali Hafed searched all over the known world of that time. He searched the Middle East and then journeyed into Europe.

Time passed, and his search became futile. By then, he had to let the servants go because his money had been depleted. He sold his camels to purchase food. After years of searching, he found himself standing between the Pillars of Hercules in Spain overlooking the sea. Ali was in rags, wretchedness, and poverty. He longed for his family, and he wanted to go home, yet he had no means to return. He was destitute because of his failure to find diamonds. As a huge wave came toward him, the poor, afflicted, suffering Ali Hafed threw himself into the sea and sank beneath its foaming crest, never to surface again.

Meanwhile, back at home, the man who had purchased Ali Hafed's farm was letting his camel drink from the garden brook. As the camel splashed its nose into the shallow water of the clear stream, Ali Hafed's successor noted a curious flash of light coming from the white sands of the stream. He pulled out a stone that had an eye of light reflecting all the hues of the rainbow. He took the stone into his house and laid it on the mantel.

Sometime later, when the same wise priest came to visit Ali Hafed's successor, he saw the beautiful stone flashing from the mantel and asked, "Where did you find this stone? It is a diamond." Excitedly, they both rushed out into the garden and stirred up the white sands of the brook with their fingers, and lo, there came up other beautiful gems, one

> after another, and some of them were even more precious than the first.
>
> This story is said to be a historically true account of the discovery of the great Golconda diamond mine. At the very time that Ali Hafed was looking for diamonds, he was living on top of one of the greatest diamond mines in the world. If he had just looked in his own backyard, he would have found his diamonds—acres of them. Instead, Ali Hafed descended into poverty and starvation, ultimately taking his own life in a strange land.[1]

Metaphorically, you have within you acres of diamonds or, in resilient terms, acres of experiences, insights, strengths, and talents that you may or may not have yet discovered. Some of the diamonds that are within your own backyard or soul include the diamonds of your nobility, the diamonds of your childlike nature, and the diamonds of your character. This chapter focuses on noble resilience. Your resilient spirit has the constant yearning and drive to harvest the diamonds of glory that you had in your first estate and magnify them in your second estate. It is the longing to become the manifestation of your foreordained blueprint.

Noble resilience in the academic world is a drive for self-worth that is imbedded deeply in the soul of every human being. Your resilient spirit is noble by nature. Your story in life is about your nobility. Nobility begins in childhood as you would plead with your parents, "Watch me!" as you were trying to do something that would please them. The incubation of nobility within childhood fantasies evolved as we are pushed into real-world expectations and maturity. Your noble drive to feel valued, important, and competent at church, school, work, and play became a major longing in your life. You yearned to feel a sense of worth and self-esteem. You long to be confident, comfortable, and significant among your family, friends, and coworkers. In your later years, you hope to leave a positive legacy.

THE DIAMONDS OF YOUR NOBLE RESILIENCE

In the pre-earth life you were among the noble and great. Your spiritual progression with its accompanying light and glory was amazing. Your mortal body at this very moment is housing magnificence. You are powerful and brilliant and amazingly righteous inside that mortal body. You are a child of God, and His spiritual DNA is shining inside of you. All your rationalizing and succumbing to mortal temptations is not the real you. You were foreordained to harvest glory during mortality. You gather bits of glory through accomplishment, purpose, altruism, and meaning. You were born to manifest the glory of God that is within each of us.

> Let your light so shine before men, that they may see your good works, and glorify your Father which is in heaven. (Matthew 5:16)

You have stored in your heart and mind memories of magnificent spiritual experiences as you walked and talked with the noble and great ones in the first estate. But part of the challenges of mortality is that you were born into this world essentially helpless and in need of nurturing from adults. You were born into this mortal world with a spirit that has millenniums of exposure to the magnificent light and glory of the Father and the Savior, but the veil essentially buried these experiences in the recesses of your unconscious mind and spirit. A glimmer of our glory is revealed to us line upon line as we read scriptures and have spiritual experiences. We know of our pre-earth greatness through the scriptures beginning with the classic reference in Abraham 3:22–23.

> Now the Lord had shown unto me, Abraham, the intelligences that were organized before the world was; and among all these there were many of the noble and great ones;
>
> And God saw these souls that they were good, and he stood in the midst of them, and he said: These I will make my rulers; for he stood among those that were spirits, and he saw that they were good; and he said unto me: Abraham, thou art one of them; thou wast chosen before thou wast born.

Another classic reference is in Jeremiah 1:5 where the Lord says, "Before I formed thee in the belly I knew thee; and before thou camest forth out of the womb I sanctified thee, and I ordained thee a prophet unto the nations."

President Joseph F. Smith observed how "we often catch a spark from the awakened memories of the immortal soul, which lights up our whole being as with the glory of our former home."[2]

Dieter F. Uchtdorf describes the first estate as follows:

> Back in that first estate, you knew with absolute certainty that God existed because you saw and heard Him. You knew Jesus Christ, who would become the Lamb of God. You had faith in Him. And you knew that your destiny was not to stay in the security of your premortal home. As much as you loved that eternal sphere, you knew you wanted and needed to embark on a journey.[3]

We often sing of this glorious first estate in the hymn "O My Father" written by Eliza R. Snow:

> For a wise and glorious purpose
> Thou hast placed me here on earth
> And withheld the recollection
> Of my former friends and birth;
> Yet ofttimes a secret something

Whispered, "You're a stranger here,"
And I felt that I had wandered
From a more exalted sphere.[4]

To personalize the reality that you are "a stranger here," you can look at your patriarchal blessing and discover the diamonds of your nobility. You learn of your rich lineage and receive hints as to your mission and purpose.

Noble resilience and the nature of your spirit may be best expressed by the noted author Marianne Williamson in her book entitled *A Return to Love* when she eloquently described the feelings of nobility:

Our deepest fear is not that we are inadequate.
Our deepest fear is that we are powerful beyond measure.
It is our light, not our darkness
That most frightens us.

We ask ourselves
Who am I to be brilliant, gorgeous, talented, fabulous?
Actually, who are you *not* to be?
You are a child of God.

Your playing small
Does not serve the world.
There's nothing enlightened about shrinking
So that other people won't feel insecure around you.

We are all meant to shine,
As children do.
We were born to make manifest
The glory of God that is within us.

It's not just in some of us;
It's in everyone.

And as we let our own light shine,
We unconsciously give other people permission to do the same.
As we're liberated from our own fear,
Our presence automatically liberates others.[5]

Williamson's introductory excerpt could have come from a general authority, for it truly captures the essence of your nobility. This chapter is focused on the exploration of the magnificence of your soul—spirit and body. We long to leave a legacy. This chapter will guide you through some ponderings and experiences that will help you uncover your innate noble nature. We will look both at the experiences your eternal spirit has had as well as your mortal nobility and the reservoir of wisdom housed within you. As an LDS culture, we are fairly unique in the religious world of our belief of the glorious first estate, yet there are hints of support in academic thought that supports the truth of glorious experience within the treasuries of your mind and spirit.

Glory in Your Mind

The famous Swedish psychologist and psychiatrist Carl Jung introduced a concept he called the *collective unconscious*.[6] He suggested that each person has a part of his or her brain that is a collection of the wisdom and experiences of all humankind. It is the wisdom of the ages. It is housed within our brains as the collective unconscious, yet is it beyond our awareness or conscious thinking. Jung proposed that through birth and genetic transfer, each generation bestowed knowledge and wisdom to the next generation. Jung's scope, without a knowledge of the first estate, helps us to understand progression and accumulation of knowledge and glory.

Housed within each person is the light and truth that is inherited from all of the previous generations. You have a reservoir of wisdom that is the combined wisdom of all the humans that have ever lived, according to Jung. The knowledge of the ages continues to crescendo as a product of one generation adding to the cumulative reservoir of knowledge to the next generation. We all stand in awe as we have witnessed the dramatic escalation of knowledge in the world even in the last couple of centuries. Can you imagine flying in a helicopter and landing near the Saints' encampment in Winter Quarters and offering them a cell phone to call their loved ones? It is the cumulative knowledge and so much more that is in reserve in our collective unconscious.

Gospel teachings also embrace this wonderful concept of the wisdom of all humankind residing within us. It should give us motivation to do our genealogy and imagine the traits of these ancestors housed within us. As you reflect upon your family history and ponder the writings of your ancestors, you can feel a resonating part of you that connects with their spirit of adventure, their altruism, and their wisdom.

You have read the stories of spiritual heroes in Church history, the Book of Mormon, and the Bible. You have read or can read about heroes in world and national history who represent the courage and hope you wish you possessed. As you feel the stirring of their spirit, you can feel it within you. You can feel the connecting joy as you resonat with their courage, humility, and honor. If you feel the warmth of the spirit-to-spirit connection, it testifies of the magnificence of your noble spirit and the richness of the reservoir of light and truth within you.

You have been there, done that, and were that in the first estate. You have within you the same qualities as those heroes. Your spirit is longing to be your noble self as you were in the first estate, but it requires becoming stronger than your mortal cravings and desires.

Jung referenced the wisdom of the ages when he spoke of archetypes, which are identities or characters that lie within us. We have the potential to access the qualities and wisdom of those characters of the ages. We can be influenced and seek the wisdom of everyone who has ever lived.

At this point, you should be seeing that within you is a genetic reservoir of identities or characters, but it is coupled with the wisdom, light, and glory of our first estate. Again, in this chapter, we are focusing on the grandeur of what is within you at this moment in time. Even though the glory may be buried under layers of mortal challenges, it is still there. We will discover in chapter 4 that we are connected to a sea of glory that is in us and all around us.

There are many skills that you can use to access the wisdom of the collective unconscious. You can train your mind using integrative health techniques, such as meditation, visualization, imagery, or music enrichment. Try the following two activities that may help you to tap into your spiritual joy of the first estate and second, access the wisdom of the ages in the second activity.

Activity: Journey to the First Estate

Reflect upon a decision or challenge you have at the moment. It may be a decision you need to make or you may be struggling with the courage to do what you need to do. It may be the need to find strength to overcome some form of addiction. When you have a moment to be alone and able to truly think about your life, get into a comfortable position, and ponder the following.

> In your mind, I want you to imagine for a moment that you are back in the first estate. Imagine as clearly as you can that you are basking in the splendor and glory of the Father. You can see and feel the light and glory emanating from Him and feel the burning in your soul as you feel your love for your Father in Heaven. You can imagine that your Father in Heaven comes to you and wraps His loving arms around you, and you almost melt as you are overcome with so much love and glory. Within that embrace with the Father, you can sense your great nobility and mission in mortal life. You are strong and powerful, having been infused with the Spirit. Spend significant time pondering your absolute

> faith in the Father and your love of the Savior. With your spirit warming your whole soul, imagine how that noble spirit would deal with the challenges that you are facing. Watch for a moment as the spiritual giant inside of you handles your situations. Watch how the qualities and virtues of honesty, influence, strength, and courage are manifest as you handle your situation. Bask in the glory of that experience, then feel the power of that spirit as you prepare to handle your life situation in your mortal experience.

It would be valuable to reflect and write your thoughts down as you consider the scenario you created and how it might apply in your life.

ACTIVITY: JOURNEY TO COLLECTIVE UNCONSCIOUS

An approach used in resiliency training is similar to the previous activity, but now you strive to access the qualities and virtues you need in life by taking a journey to heroes in your mind or, as per Carl Jung, your collective unconscious. Again, with a situation in the back of your mind that needs resolution, think about the people in your ancestry or the history of humankind that may have encountered similar problems. These are people that had the humility, compassion, courage, leadership, or fighting spirit that you need for your current life situation.

One of the wonderful blessings of modern scriptures is that you can find heroes throughout them. You can review their capacities to respond to challenges and learn how they exemplified powerful qualities you wish you had. King Benjamin, Mary, Samuel, David, Mosiah, Nephi, Sarah, Enoch, or numerous other heroes. Perhaps your hero comes from one of the Saints who was in the handcart companies that demonstrated amazing faith and grit. Desirable thriving qualities come as well from the great people in world or American history such as George Washington, Deborah Gannett, Davy Crockett, Eleanor Roosevelt, Benjamin Franklin, or Rosa Parks. Perhaps you are thinking of a person of wisdom and compassion, and Abraham Lincoln or Mother Teresa come to mind. Perhaps it is one of your ancestors.

For this activity, take some time to ponder one or two resilient heroes that you know, knew, or read about that exemplified unbreakable qualities that you are hoping for to deal with a life challenge.

> In your imagination, I want you to take a journey into your collective unconscious mind. Fantasize that you have become very tiny and will enter your brain, which appears to be a vast auditorium. There is a path that winds through the great auditorium of your mind.

Imagine that you are walking along the endless path and there are branches along the way that lead to different people. You will see the people at the end of the branching paths as you might imagine them.

As you walk along the path, you decide to visit one of the people in your ancestry or a famous person in history. Pick a person from whom you would like to seek counsel. Imagine yourself walking up the path and meeting the person you have sought for counsel and as an exemplar of the qualities you are seeking. As you arrive at his or her location, imagine what the situation is and how he or she might look. Imagine that the hero embraces you, and you sit down to talk. You can feel the qualities that you desire from this hero. Imagine the conversation you might have. What wisdom will be given to you? Feel the qualities the person exemplifies radiating toward you, and feel yourself becoming like your exemplar. You feel his or her character and goodness as you assume his or her strengths. Rehearse in your mind how you might engage your challenge or decision with the acquired qualities. Enjoy the conversation for a few moments. As you end the imagery, keep the power of the qualities within you.

Becoming Noble in the Second Estate

There are two interdependent workings that help you to experience your noble resilience. The first is through personal accomplishment, and the second is through altruism or service.

Personal accomplishment begins as an infant, and you progress from total dependence upon an adult to gradually becoming independent. You feel an infusion of joy and excitement when you take your first steps. You celebrate accomplishment when you learn to ride a bike. You get warm feelings when you pass a test in school. Throughout life, you increase your nobility by receiving Scout and Young Women awards. You receive it when you graduate from high school and college and when you get your first job. You feel the thrill of glory as you find success in the professional world or in raising spiritually based families. Perhaps even more important is to feel the joy as the scriptures become alive. As you continue to read scriptures to accomplish spiritual goals, you find yourself evolving from just being inspired by the stories to finding spiritual diamonds in a single verse that cause you to ponder, finding great peace in the meaning.

Personal accomplishment is important to give you confidence to be able to serve others, which brings even more joy. Simplistically, yet so profound, is the act of helping someone during a difficult time by listening, helping, or validating. When you perform a service, expressions of gratitude fill your soul. The acts fill your soul with glory, which add to your nobility.

The message of altruistic service in the gospel is clear. Members receive callings to be able to serve, allowing them to feel the infusions of glory with each service rendered whether it is teaching a lesson or passing the sacrament. Members can feel the infusion of light, and they continue to enhance their nobility through the progressive harvesting of glory.

Purpose and Meaning

Two subjects often discussed in the psychological and philosophical worlds of academia are purpose and meaning. What really is the purpose of life? What is the meaning in all of this in the world? This is an easy answer for members of the Church. Your purpose in life is to fulfill your foreordination. You do it by accomplishment and by service to others. Your meaning is life is the product of purpose. As you act upon your drive for personal accomplishment and then to serve others, meaning is the infusion of the spirit, light, truth, and glory in the aftermath of that service or accomplishment. You conquer life challenges with a noble resilient spirit and living with purpose and meaning.

Notes

1. Russell H. Conwell, "Acres of Diamonds," Temple University, accessed March 28, 2017, https://www.temple.edu/about/history-and-traditions/acres-diamonds.
2. Joseph F. Smith, *Gospel Doctrine* (Salt Lake City: Deseret Book, 1977), 13–14.
3. Dieter F. Uchtdorf, "Your Wonderful Journey Home," *Ensign*, May 2013, 126.
4. "O My Father," *Hymns*, no. 292.
5. Marianne Williamson, *A Return to Love: Reflections on the Principles of "A Course in Miracles"* (New York: HarperCollins, 1992), 190.
6. Carl Jung, "The Concept of the Collective Unconscious," in *The Collected Works of C. G. Jung*, vol. 9, *The Archetypes and the Collective Unconscious* (Princeton: Princeton University Press, 1968), 44.

3

The Diamonds of Your Resilient Spirit

Childlike and Character Resilience

Even though we are born into this world with no recollection of our pre-earth glory, still we are blessed with innate diamonds that help us to become resilient spirits. In mortality, we have innate gifts and strengths that help us to become unbreakable in times of challenge if we use them. Two of those spiritual gifts are your childlike and character natures.

Many of us are familiar with the enchanting little book by Robert Fulghum entitled *All I Really Need to Know I Learned in Kindergarten.* He states, "Wisdom was not at the top of the graduate-school mountain, but there in the sandpile at Sunday School." He posed that the resilient qualities of sharing, playing, not hitting other people, not taking things that aren't yours, and cleaning up your own mess, among others, are the keys to joyful living. He suggested that we "live a balanced life—learn some and think some and draw and paint and sing and dance and play and work every day some." He continues, "When you go out into the world, watch out for traffic, hold hands, and stick together. Be aware of wonder. . . . And then remember the Dick-and-Jane books and the first word you learned—the biggest of all—LOOK. Everything you need to know is in there somewhere."[1]

Even though we have a veil between us and our rich experiences in the first estate, still we can see from Fulghum's clever insight that we are born with a resilient spirit, even in kindergarten. You can use the energy from your childlike nature to become unbreakable with a resilient spirit. Even though you have forgotten your amazing nobility as described in chapter 2, by reading scriptures, receiving a patriarchal blessing, and absorbing inspiring talks from Church leaders, you can still catch a glimpse of your glorious first estate. You begin to realize that much of your purpose in life is to discover, nurture, and become the embodiment of your resilient spirit. Beginning with your first days on earth as an infant, you were clueless as to anything of a spiritual nature and were focused on the basics of survival. Adults could see your pure, radiant spirit, but you just wanted a bottle and have someone change your diaper.

As you grew older and progressed physically, mentally, and spiritually, you found yourself at Primary and junior Sunday School with some energizing and sometimes uncontrollable drives to be noticed, and you likely acted as most children do. It is within this extraordinary bundle of childlike energy that you can rediscover and harness your vitality to conquer life challenges. One only needs to be in a Primary class of a dozen six- and seven-year-olds for a short time to be overwhelmed with their excitement and energy. When that boundless energy is applied to life challenges, it can provide the motivation and persistence to thrive.

It is unfortunate many adults have buried their childlike spirit, not recognizing that it is a powerful force that helps to unearth their hidden noble spirits during this second estate. Your childlike nature infuses you with zeal in fulfilling your foreordination. In our wards, we sometimes stand in admiration as we witness the energy and drive of some members of the Church as they are engaged in their family, church, and professional duties. We have also seen members who may have lost the glory in their countenances because their energy and drives have been sapped and drained when they live outside of moral teachings of the gospel. We will discuss the ebb and flow of spiritual energy that is generated from one's childlike nature and drained in the wake of character compromises.

The Energizing Childlike Resilient Spirit

Too often members of the Church ignore the powerful implications and opportunities for progression that are implied from the Savior's statement in Matthew 18:3 where He states, "Verily I say unto you, except ye be converted, and become as little children, ye shall not enter into the kingdom of heaven." Again, in Matthew 19:14, we read, "But Jesus said, suffer the little children, and forbid them not, to come unto me: for of such is the kingdom of heaven." Most of us read over these two scriptures and simply ponder within ourselves that we need to be innocent like a child to enter the kingdom of heaven. But it is so much more than just trying to be "innocent like a child."

We can begin to open the door to examining the depth of these two scriptures when we consider the sometimes alarming honesty and openness of a child. They tell it like it is. They have implicit faith that many adults wish they had. They are nonjudgmental and will play with anyone regardless of culture, race, or physical challenge. Childlike resilience taps into the abundance of vitality that is found in play, laughter, fun, adventures, and being creative. Your innate childlike, resilient diamonds can help you conquer life challenges, help you to progress, and assist you in catching glimpses of your noble nature. Childlike resilience is the rich reserve of energy in every soul that can be channeled into overcoming life's challenges with hope and optimism.

As you reflect upon your childhood years, you may remember how you worked through life experiences with natural coping skills. When you were upset—such as when another child took a toy from you or your parent had you stop playing—you recovered in a very short amount of time. You rarely held grudges. You were not afraid to try new activities and learn new games. You would jump from trees or high places for the thrill. You were creative, loved to draw, and were skilled at self-entertainment. Your imagination was vivid as you played with imaginary friends and dolls. Cars and animals could be made of anything. When you played with dolls or tinker toys, you were totally engaged. In current psychology, this experience of having your body, mind, and spirit all engaged in an activity is called a *flow state*.[2] Many modern-day positive approaches to therapy endorse mindfulness, or being in the present, as an important skill. As kids, being present was easy.

What happened to us since childhood? Unfortunately, as we age many of us begin to play "grown up" and bury these wonderful childlike qualities. Your resilient spirit is a childlike spirit with qualities that are still within you but might be suffocating under layers of challenging life experiences and adult expectations. Many of us try to become an ideal LDS exemplar and sadly lose ourselves in multitasking and following rigid schedules, unable to enjoy our childlike spirit because of so many demands.

To be as a little child is to engage in each new challenge as a creative adventure. Family home evening should include play and humor even if only adults are attending. Resilient saints brainstorm creative new approaches to overcoming life challenges. Why worry and feel hurt about things you cannot control for long periods of time when you can be as a child and quickly shake it off and move on? You can live your life with a resilient spirit if you can find meaning when the Savior is speaking of children and says, "Of such is the kingdom of heaven" (Matthew 19:14). Sometimes when life challenges are ready to break you, simply sing "'Give,' Said the Little Stream," and it will remind you to attack your problems with a sense of childlike adventure.

To be unbreakable, it is important to rediscover your childlike qualities and learn to use them responsibly in adult life. Childlike resilience encompasses the yearnings for adventure, play, and fun. To begin, let me take you through an exercise that should help you to remember some pleasant memories from childhood. It is from these memories that you will be able to discover and use your childlike resilient spirit.

Childlike Reflection

In pursuit of your innate resilient spirit, let's start by exploring the qualities of your childlike nature.

Step 1

In your imagination, go back to your childhood and remember happy times. I recognize that some of you may have had difficulties in your childhood, but hopefully, there were some times when you were able to play and have fun as children should. Write down five or six of your favorite things that you did as a child. Before you choose, let me help trigger your memory by asking a few questions that may have been associated with your childhood experiences. I also recognize that some of you, as converts, did not attend Primary, so I will try and make these trigger questions apply to everyone.

- Did you like to play in water (bathtubs, pools, lakes, the ocean, water hoses, squirt guns, water balloons)?
- Did you like playing with friends (clubs, sleepovers, group games)?
- Did you like to travel (family vacations, amusement parks, games in the car, riding in trains or planes)?
- What childhood games and toys did you like to play with (dolls; electric trains; Monopoly; chemistry sets; craft sets; playing house; Red Rover; Mother May I?; Red Light, Green Light)?
- What active games did you like to play (tetherball, kickball, dodge ball, climbing on the monkey bars)?
- When did you feel safe and comfortable (in someone's arms, when alone in your room, in the yard, at church)?
- Did you like adventures (sleeping out in the yard, hiking, riding bikes, playing night games)?
- Who did you like to visit (a grandparent, a neighbor, an uncle or aunt, a friend)?
- What did you like to create (drawing, painting, building with blocks, other types of art)?

At the end of this exercise are some columns for you to complete. In column 1 write the activities that you like to do from step 1.

Step 2

After you have identified five or six things that you liked to do, consider the energizing childlike qualities that you felt when you were doing those activities. To clarify this step, consider the following example from my own life:

> When I was a kid, we lived on a small five-acre homestead near San Diego. We had a couple of horses, raised a few chickens, raised our own beef, and had a huge garden. At that time, we had to build

> a septic tank, which required digging a huge hole in the ground, and after a tank was buried, there still remained a wonderful dirt pile. I used to spend hours out on the pile of dirt by myself, building communities. I had some toy cars, and I would build roads and dig little caves for the houses. It was a beautiful creation. Then when it would rain, it was a blessing, because that meant I got to fluff the dirt and rebuild the community in a whole new way.

One of my favorite childhood activities was digging in a dirt pile. Why did I enjoy it? It was fun. It was creative. It was play. It triggered my imagination. It was mindful. Therefore, in column 2, I would write the feelings of creativity, fun, play, etc.

STEP 3

After you have identified the childlike urges that come from the human spirit, ask yourself, "What am I doing now, as an adult, to fulfill those same needs?" In column 3 under step 3 you can write your responses.

As I pondered what I am doing now to fulfill my creative needs and trigger my imagination, I realized that my work as a professor is creative and imaginative. Even writing this book is like playing in a dirt pile. I am trying to look at an adventurous way to apply the plan of salvation in my own life and the daily lives of Latter-day Saints. It is fun to dig roads and make tunnels to discover ways to access the sea of glory in which we live. So how do I fulfill my creative needs as an adult? My "dirt pile" is now my computer. I love to ponder the "so what?" the "what does it mean?" and the "how do people apply this?" to everything. I'm just making roads and digging tunnels in a beautiful dirt pile of amazing gospel treasures. FYI—I still love to sit in a freshly dumped pile of dirt and feel its warmth in my hands and shape a road or two.

Step 1 Activities I Did as a Kid	**Step 2** Qualities or Feelings from Doing It	**Step 3** What Am I Doing Now?
1.	1.	1.
2.	2.	2.
3.	3.	3.
4.	4.	4.
5.	5.	5.
6.	6.	6.

As you ponder how to apply your childlike yearnings to enrich your resilient spirit, you can reflect upon the previous activity and then consider if there are other childlike qualities that may help you to become unbreakable.

When the Savior stated, "Suffer little children, and forbid them not, to come unto me: for of such is the kingdom of heaven" (Matthew 19:14), new images of that kingdom may come to mind. Could the kingdom of heaven in the pre-earth estate or even after our resurrection to one of the degrees of glory include the qualities of being childlike? Could the celestial kingdom be fun? Could we laugh and play? Could we still have adventures? Could we will still find the joy and excitement of doing creative activities? Why can't our second estate be childlike?

> *Please note that I am not saying *childish* but *childlike.* Anytime your sense of play, creativity, or adventure infringes on the nobility of someone else or hurts their feelings, you have lost the spirit of being as a little child.

These invigorating childlike drives can help you to become unbreakable as you use the animating childlike qualities to thrive through life challenges. To further help you reflect upon how you can enrich the roles you have in life with a childlike spirit, you can ponder the following suggestions. Remember that part of your noble foreordination, as described in chapter 2, is to touch lives. These suggestions should help you to ponder what is buried underneath your need to be a serious adult, a parenting role model, and an LDS exemplar. These are all good, but each adult role can be enriched with a childlike quality. Hopefully you will unearth an exuberant bubbling resilient spirit that wants to engage in life.

- **Resilient Spirit of Adventure:** Engage challenges, problems, and opportunities with a childlike sense of adventure. Feel the spirit of conquering the challenge as you would climbing a mountain. Take reasonable risks. Try new activities. Meet new people. Learn new skills. Step out of homeostasis as per the plan of salvation and resiliency model from chapter 1.

- **Resilient Spirit of Fun and Play:** Play in your life for balance and for your own wellbeing. Try to make conquering your challenges fun. Having fun will help to connect with family, with church groups, and in your profession. View your challenges with a game-like attitude.
- **Resilient Sprit of Creativity:** Rather than responding to problems and challenges with the same approach, ponder some creative approach to react differently. Even though your life challenges are difficult, brainstorming new ways to deal with it creatively can put excitement into your solution.
- **Resilient Spirit of Learning and Being Teachable:** Being as a child is to learn continually and feel the childlike insatiable appetite to learn and ask the questions of "Why?" "How?" and "So What?" You will experience a warm feeling of excitement as you take on your life challenges with a new approach that you have just learned. Enjoy the playground of learning and progressing.
- **Resilient Spirit of Humor:** Try to see the humor in a challenge. Granted, at the time it is often difficult to do, but as you reflect upon past challenges, you can usually find the humor if the incident passed without permanent harm. Isn't it interesting that when you tell the story of a difficult past experience to family and friends that often you end up laughing about it? For example, perhaps you have experienced a time when you spilled your food or drink on yourself in a social setting. At the moment, you were horrified. But upon retelling, it becomes a funny story of how you tried to cover the stains on the clothes with a napkin and walked out of the room, covering yourself to get to the bathroom. Your story of challenge becomes funny with the passing of time. Try to find the humor in the event

as you think, "Oh my, I can't wait to tell my friends what happened—they won't believe it!"

- **Resilient Spirit of Spontaneity:** Spiritual prompts sometimes just jump into our minds. It may be as simple as when you are passing someone in your ward and a thought jumps into your mind to give a complement. As a young boy, I still remember a sweet sister made a quick comment as we were walking out of church, simply saying, "Buzz, you have such a great smile." It was just a random spontaneous comment, and she really had no idea the impact that had on my nature. I smiled a lot more after that. Sometimes a spontaneous feeling that you should change the way you travel home for newness or what could end up with a purpose. Spontaneity can add spice to a normally routine day.
- **Resilient Spirit of Genuineness:** Have you pondered the age-old question, "Who am I?" To this point in the book, I hope you have pondered the nature of your amazing spirit in the first estate and now your childlike nature. Be true to yourself to have the full spirit of who you are to conquer life challenges.

You may want to write about some of your thoughts as to how the resilient spirit of adventure, fun, play, creativity, learning, humor, spontaneity, and genuineness can enrich the roles you have in life.

By pondering and acting upon how the kingdom of God can be childlike, you add to the spirit of your family, ward, and neighborhood. When applied correctly, enhancing and activating your childlike nature can help you discover the renewed energy that comes from finding humor in life events. It can help you to see life as a challenge or adventure. You will be able to use your childlike creativity to develop skills to increase your energy to conquer your challenges. You can try the following activity that may heighten your awareness of your resilient spirit.

Childlike Quality Breathing

Think of a challenge you may have in your life. Perhaps you struggle to read your scriptures. Perhaps you lack enthusiasm about your calling in the Church. Perhaps you need to mend a disagreement with another member of your ward or a family member. Perhaps you need to make some changes in your lifestyle and adopt some healthier habits. Now try the following:

1. Identify one of the childlike yearnings as described above that you think would help you deal with your selected challenge.
2. Get into a comfortable position and breathe naturally.
3. Breathe in through your nose and out through your mouth. Breathe diaphragmatically by letting your stomach rise and fall with each breath.
4. With each inhalation, imagine that each breath contains little particles of the childlike quality you identified. For example, you may be imagining little particles of adventure with each inhalation.
5. As you breathe in, feel a gradually increasing sense of the quality you identified. You can imagine it filling your lungs and then moving slowly throughout the rest of your body.
6. Continue to breathe in the quality, but now, with each exhalation, begin to expel all the barriers to fulfilling that quality. For example, with adventure, your exhalation

might be ridding yourself of fears. You breathe in adventure and exhale fear.

7. Continue to breathe in the feeling of your chosen quality, and then let it go to your glorious spirit, and then your mind, and then your whole soul.
8. As you feel the quality within you, you may want to apply it to a real-life challenge. Sense how you can feel it helping you. Imagine that with each inhalation, you can effectively make a life situation better with the quality. For example, imagine that you use an adventurous spirit to successfully bring your family closer.

Childlike Imagination and Daydreaming

When you were a child, your imagination allowed you to escape to far-off destinations and live in fantasy worlds. That same daydreaming skill can allow you to find joy in life now, even in difficult circumstances. As a child, you could see colors, hear sounds, taste foods, touch animals, and smell the roses in your wild imaginations. With those same skills, you can use your imagination to identify ways to make situations better. For example, when you are experiencing stress from a life challenge, your muscles will be tense, your heart rate will be rapid, and your breathing will be labored. You can stop for a moment and let your imagination take you to stress-free places.

Reflecting upon chapter 2, you can escape to the love and peace of your spiritual world that is inside of you with your imagination. You can imagine someplace that is fun. You can be at Disneyland, in the mountains, or at the beach. You can imagine that you are singing songs and enjoying great company around a campfire. You can imagine being in the temple. Your imagination will allow you to walk along stressful streets in the city yet feel like you are strolling along a beach in Hawaii. You can imagine that people in other cars are friends and you can smile at them. Your ability to imagine is a gift from childhood that lets you create wonderful scenarios and enjoy them along the journey of becoming an unbreakable saint. Try this activity.

> With your amazing ability to imagine, take the opportunity to visualize a challenge in your life. As you see the see the challenge in your mind, use your imagination to make it as real as possible in your mind by adding the sounds, smells, sights, tastes, and physical feelings. Now, conquer the challenge in your mind with your childlike resilient spirit. For example, imagine yourself conquering your challenge with a sense of creativity. You can write your thoughts down and find new energy to be resilient in your challenge.
>
> You can then try to use your imagination with your other childlike resilient drives as well. For example, you can consider your challenge like playing a game of chess. You can plot a strategy and then think about how the challenge may respond with a move. You can use your imaginary game to plot your strategy to conquer your challenge.

Childlike Qualities with Current Challenges

Many times, we approach life challenges with worry, sadness, and hopelessness. The resilient spirit that is within you views life's challenges a different way. Insurmountable tasks or strained relationships are viewed from the childlike view as opportunities for creativity, adventure, and reasonable risk taking. Consider the following story:

> I remember a time when I had to discipline my son, who was about eight years old at the time. He had been teasing and picking on his younger sister until she came to me in tears. The conversation I had was calm and collected in a moment of parental wisdom, and I suggested to him that he sit in a corner and

think about better ways to play with his sister. He begrudgingly walked to the corner with his head hanging low. He sat down with a long look on his face. I told him that I would be back in a few minutes and we would discuss better options for playing with his sister. I walked out of the room and tiptoed to a vantage point where I could watch him undetected.

It seemed clear that this opportunity to reflect upon his wrongdoing was working for him, and I felt smug that my intervention exemplified ideal parenting. For about a minute, he sat there thinking about something. I got a smile on my face and anxiously awaited our opportunity to talk. I let him ponder for a few more minutes to make sure enough time had passed for the disciplining to have real meaning.

As I peered from my hiding place, I noticed that he started to rub his fingers through the carpet. He found a little thread. He grabbed the thread between his thumb and finger and started moving it along the wall like a little worm. The wall was textured, so the worm had numerous passageways to explore. He then reached into his pocket and pulled out a little pebble he had picked up during his outdoor adventures earlier that day. Now the worm began to chase the pebble through the textured matrix on the wall. He started making noises for the characters in this adventure. My best read was that the thread was a snake, as evidenced by the hissing sound, and the little pebble was his sister, based upon the falsetto voice of the pebble. Occasionally the snake would catch her and scare her, and then she (the pebble), would escape through the matrix screaming.

My moment as a parenting genius was dashed within four minutes as my son continued to pester his sister, even if it was just in his imagination.

Difficult situations can be softened when you choose to approach challenges with your childlike nature. From the plan of salvation model or resiliency process described in chapter 1, you know that when life events happen, you will initially feel hurt, loss, guilt, or fear. But during the disruption, you can access your childlike sense of glory in the form of creativity, adventure, and hope. In the face of adult challenges, consider that childlike qualities can lead to insightful moments. Stories abound of people in difficult situations using their childlike qualities to survive.

> Mike, after being married for twenty-five years, found himself divorced and alone in a two-bedroom apartment. He felt lonely and rejected, and he didn't think anyone would ever want to be with him again. He was fifty-four years old. After work, he would just go home, hide out in his little apartment, and feel sorry for himself. He finally realized that this was no life—staying in his disruption. He wanted to create a new life but didn't know how to do so at his age.
>
> Mike forced himself to go to a single-adult fireside. He showed up late and was forced to take one empty seat behind a support pillar in the Joseph Smith Building. He could not see the speaker. The speaker was not the best he had ever heard. Mike made some smart-aleck comments to the woman next to him. Afterward, he walked out with the woman and met her friends. He visited with the women for a few minutes and got the phone number of one of them.
>
> On the way home he began to brainstorm and pondered, "What are some of the things I used to like to do in high school and college?" He recalled that he loved to dance. He liked hiking. He loved to go to the mountains and play games like Capture the Flag. He knew a couple of other men in his stake who were single and were feeling sorry for themselves as well and had lost their childlike natures.

> Mike convinced the three women he had met at the fireside and his guy friends that life was too short to sit around and not have any fun. He invited the women and his guy friends to his apartment for a chance to get acquainted. Mike brought out games, and the whole group had a great time.
>
> The word spread, and soon around thirty people would get together to play games, go to dances, ski, and even play Capture the Flag in the mountains. They went on many adventures together.
>
> Mike had rediscovered his innate spiritual child-like resilience and again found joy in life. As a side bar and over time, Mike met and married a wonderful woman who had joined this playful group.

Mike's childlike longing for enjoyment helped him to conquer the challenge of his loneliness and sadness. He also accessed his noble spirit with the drive of harvesting glory in mortality and reached out to help others who were also needing to create a way to be happy. Being as a child became the avenue for him to rediscover a happy married life.

Roles with Your Childlike Nature

Most people act and behave in ways that are dictated by their roles. You may play the roles of priesthood leader, Relief Society counselor, Sunday School teacher, youth leader, family member, professional, or neighbor. These roles may lead you to act differently from how you would really like to act. Many people are afraid to be genuine. The following exercise first asks you to make a list of roles that you have in life. Include anytime a given situation leads you to behave in a different way. That is a role. For example, your parenting role with a nine-month-old baby may be different from your role when parenting a seventeen-year-old teenager.

ROLES

1. List as many roles as you can in the chart to the right (spouse, son or daughter, parent, worker, neighbor, church member, volunteer, friend, etc.).
2. Describe how the roles could be better if you were to incorporate some of your childlike qualities into those roles. For example, how can you create experiences to understand gospel principles as an adventure? How can you make your role as a visiting or home teacher more fun or playful? What if you were able to help people in your world laugh? How could you make your daily responsibilities more adventurous or fun? As you consider the roles in your life, use your imagination to embrace the childlike qualities that would make your roles better. In your mind, rehearse the experience of becoming more childlike and imagine how each role could be enriched with them. Describe how your roles evolve in the chart following the example:

THE ROLE	ROLE IMPROVED WITH CHILDLIKE QUALITIES
1. As a friend to a member who lost his wife a year ago in an accident	1. Take him with me to explore the caves in the nearby mountains
2.	2.
3.	3.
4.	4.
5.	5.
6.	6.
7.	7.

To continue my story after being hit by a car, let me share some of my childlike adventures.

> After three months of rehabilitating at home, I returned to work at the university in early March. I was still in a wheelchair, and the eight pins were still in my lower legs. My administrative assistant, Lu Jean, had been very concerned with the ordeal I had been through. Many people at work had donated blood on my behalf. Everyone became very motherly and protective in the office. My childlike sense of adventure and play was churning inside of me, yet I was still trapped in a wheelchair. I tried to get back to my normal routine and started working on projects. When writing an article, I knew that I would need some references for the project. While I was appreciative of everyone's concerns, the excitement of going to the library by myself seemed freeing and fun. I left my office and wheeled past Lu Jean at her desk, simply saying, "I'm going to the library," and sped out the door as quickly as I could without hearing her response.
>
> My office was located at the top of a sidewalk that had a downhill grade of some five hundred yards. At the bottom of the grade was the library. The fresh air seemed to ignite my soul. I started rolling down the hill as Lu Jean came flying out of the office, yelling, "Dr. Richardson! Dr. Richardson! I'll get your references. You shouldn't do this!" Too late; I was rollin'. I accelerated and began to go faster and faster until the wheelchair started to shimmy and shake. The thrill of letting loose filled my soul, and I was exuberant! Even the fear of potentially crashing felt good for a while, until I realized that wheelchairs were not meant to go as fast as mine was moving. With my whole body vibrating, I tried to slow the wheelchair down with my bare hands on the wheels,

> with modest effect. While rolling down the hill, I waved to students as they jumped out of the way. As I went flying by, they just giggled to see the runaway professor in the wheelchair. I finally got to the bottom of the hill without crashing. What a rush! It felt so good to do something crazy and fun because it had been bottled up inside me for months. It was great to be free from the mothering.
>
> Upon reflection, I realized that I took a serious risk, and I could have hurt myself and others, but oh, it was energizing! After doing my research in the library, wheeling up the hill was more laborious. I had forgotten how out of shape I was. I would push the wheels for about one hundred feet and then have to rest. Then I would push for another one hundred feet. Students were gracious in offering to help, but I would simply respond that I was doing my aerobics.

The Unbreakable Diamonds of Your Character Resilience

Character resilience is the yearning to live within the peace that comes from abiding by the commandments and being in harmony with your innate sense of what is right or wrong. It is the Spirit of Christ. The conclusion of this chapter is not about admonishing you to live the commandments, because you hear that regularly at church. It is about helping you understand how that by living within the laws of God, you will have ample energy to become unbreakable. You learned of the thirteenth article of faith when you were introduced to the Church or in Primary.

> We believe in being honest, true, chaste, benevolent, virtuous, and in doing good to all men; indeed, we may say that we follow the admonition of Paul—We believe all things, we hope all things, we have endured many things, and hope to be able to endure all things.

> If there is anything virtuous, lovely, or of good report or praiseworthy, we seek after these things.

You have embraced the beatitudes from the Sermon on the Mount that taught you to be honest, humble, moral, giving, loving, and other highlights of great character. In order to be unbreakable as a resilient saint and to thrive through life challenges, you need ample energy, but that energy can be sapped if you live outside of the commandments. It is interesting that the principles we learn in the gospel such as honesty, integrity, and kindness are evident in almost every philosophy and theology on the planet. It is part of the human birthright. When you live within the commandments you have energy, and when you sin, you have energy drain.

The ebb and flow of the childlike exuberance and engagement in life is evident when we live the teachings of the Church. The spiritual flow that comes from the childlike fervor and vigor can be used for conquering great challenges; however it can also quickly be dampened by the ebb of character compromises. To provide a metaphor for this phenomenon, I recall a story when I was in the Young Men program in our ward and we took our canoes to the Colorado River.

> The Young Men in our ward decided that we would build canoes with the eventual goal of paddling down the Colorado River. Over the winter months we built the canoes with slates from fruit crates and covered them with canvas and fiberglass paint. They were heavy.
>
> The first time we tried to venture down the Colorado River was in late spring. We put the canoes on top of our cars and trucks, left El Cajon, crossed the desert of the Imperial Valley, and arrived at the river. We unloaded our canoes, put them on the banks of the river, placed our backpacks with supplies in the canoes, put on lifejackets, and ventured down the river.

> The water was swift, which made the trip more exciting and challenging. We had fun riding the rapids and dropping down small waterfalls as well as riding the wake of some of the boats that would pass us, as they too were enjoying the full river that was over a hundred yards wide in several places.
>
> After a couple of days of riding the river, leaders picked us up several miles downriver. When we returned home with our dramatic stories, we immediately began to plan a return trip. Late in the summer, we ventured again to take on the mighty Colorado River and we returned with our canoes.
>
> On the drive out, we noticed the lush and beautiful watermelon and cantaloupe fields. We saw rows and rows of date palms. We could see the irrigation canals that were feeding these beautiful oases in the desert. When we got to the river, we were surprised and disappointed. Rather than the river flowing with an abundance of water, there was but a stream. We still took our canoes down the river that had become a stream, but it was more laborious for us. We often had to stop and lift our canoes over the sandbars that surfaced in the wake of the scarcity of water.
>
> When we asked our leaders what had happened, they explained to us that the water had been diverted to tributaries and canals to nourish the watermelons, palms, and cantaloupes we had passed on our way out.

So it is with our lives. All the adventure and enthusiasm to engage in life challenges can be quickly dampened if our energy is diverted to deal with the grief and guilt that sucks the energy from our resilient spirits. Living with a resilient spirit within the moral guidelines of the Church brings a purer connection with the Holy Spirit. It is as though your spirit is a prism that absorbs the glory from God, and it passes through you cleanly to radiate that glory in your countenance. If the prism is clouded by violating your character code, the light is dimmed and the energy you need to progress through the resilient journey is compromised. You end up trying to navigate the joyful spirit of life's rivers with very little water.

So many of the scriptures are about keeping your rivers full and prisms clear of the opaqueness of character compromises. As you read the pleading of the prophets and apostles over the centuries, you can sense the great wisdom of assuring that you have an abundance of spiritual waters. Here are a few examples:

> Use boldness, but not overbearance; and also see that ye bridle all your passions, that ye may be filled with love; see that ye refrain from idleness. (Alma38:12)
>
> And the cares of this world, and the deceitfulness of riches, and the lusts of other things entering in, choke the word, and it becometh unfruitful. (Mark 4:19)
>
> Behold, I say unto you, wickedness never was happiness. (Alma 41:10)
>
> The truth shall make you free. (John 8:32)

In a talk entitled "Purity Precedes Power," Elder M. Russell Ballard stated, "Remember, young men, that purity precedes power. The Lord said, 'But purify your hearts before me; and then go ye into all the world, and preach my gospel unto every creature who has not received it' (D&C 112:28)."[3]

Each of these scriptures and many more talk of having an abundance of water in our spiritual rivers to truly enjoy our mortal progression. The flowing waters of happiness, boldness, and the ability to preach should not be diverted into the tributaries of character compromises and sin. To sense the feelings of the spiritual bleeding that occurs with compromising your character, consider times in your life such as these:

- Lying and then trying to cover it up
- Compromising your integrity by not doing what you say you will do
- Telling off-color jokes
- Gossiping and demeaning a brother or sister.

From what we read in the Bible and in the history of the world, these character qualities have been prevalent since the beginning. The immutable and foundational part of our resilient spirit should be as constant as the stars in the heavens. For happiness and progression, your resilient journey in life needs to be guided by your sense of honesty, integrity, and honor.

The resilient spirit engages life with a childlike vigor and a sense of adventure of discovering your amazing spiritual nobility. I will never forget the amazing character example from our dear neighbor and ward member during the time of my accident. Her demonstration of kindness and her nobility continues to touch my heart to this day.

> It was Christmas Eve, and I had taken a bad turn and began to slip into a deeper and deeper coma for no apparent reason. After spending the entire day at my bedside, my wife had left the hospital to go home to get some rest.
>
> Driving home with a heavy heart, the thought of four children at home expecting a traditional Christmas celebration began to weigh on her. My poor worried mother was home watching the children, and still, the weight of Christmas seemed overwhelming to my wife. Both my wife and mother were exhausted and emotionally drained. As she had done during the previous four days, with my mother's help, my wife found an inner strength to continue to carry everyone though this ordeal.
>
> It was dark when she arrived home, and the children would be hungry. As she drove in the driveway, a dear neighbor and member of the ward, Laurie,

> approached the front door. Laurie was holding a large covered tray with a complete dinner inside for the whole family. As my wife got out of the car and approached Laurie, a warm greeting and smile from this dear sister melted her heart. My wife said, "Why are you doing this on Christmas Eve? Shouldn't you be home with your own family?"
>
> With a spirit of love in her voice, Laurie responded softly and compassionately, "What do you think Christmas is all about?"
>
> I can rarely reflect upon this experience without becoming very emotional and teary. Why did Laurie, with a household of children of her own, give up part of her family celebration to prepare and deliver a Christmas meal for a family that was struggling? Here is a Saint who listened to the prompting of the Spirit and gave in the season of giving.

Laurie experienced an infusion of glory as she delivered her meal. Reflecting upon where we are in building your unbreakable resilient spirit, you know that you have an amazing noble spirit that keeps trying to have you fulfill your glorious foreordination. You are blessed with spirit from your childlike nature, in addition to the other sources identified in this book, and you can maintain your energy if you live within the qualities and virtues outlined in the commandments. In the next chapter, to help fortify you even more, we will explore the power of the world of glory, light, and energy in which you live that will help you to become unbreakable and thrive through life challenges.

NOTES

1. Robert Fulghum, *All I Really Need to Know I Learned in Kindergarten: Uncommon Thoughts on Common Things* (New York: Villard Books, 1990), 6–7.
2. Mihaly Csíkszentmihályi, *Finding Flow: The Psychology of Engagement with Everyday Life* (New York: Basic Books, 1997).
3. M. Russell Ballard, "Purity Precedes Power," *Ensign*, November 1990.

4

THE RESILIENT SPIRIT IN A SEA OF GLORY

ECOLOGICAL AND UNIVERSAL RESILIENCE

You are walking, living, and breathing in a sea of glory that is within you and all around you—you can bathe yourself in that illuminating glory that will assure that you are unbreakable and able to conquer life challenges. Resilient spirits are those that harvest the glory in their worlds and harness the amazing love, wisdom, truth, light, guidance, and power that conquers life challenges.

To become an unbreakable saint, you need wisdom and strength beyond your normal capacity to be able to conquer your life challenges. As you make decisions and work through difficult times, the warm comfort of light and truth gives you courage to do what you need to do. In this chapter we will explore the amazing nature and power of glory in your world and the universe. Later in chapter 6, we will learn skills to access the sea of glory that will help to fortify your resilient spirit, but for now, we will examine some of the wisdom from a selection of sciences that explain how powerful the sea of glory can potentially be in our lives.

In the troughs of the limited vision and capacity that is inherent in mortality and during times of feeling discouraged or hopeless, we often fall to our knees and pray for help to have wisdom and strength to conquer life challenges. We know that the power of God can help us. We pray for relief from emotional and physical pain. We seek for wisdom that we know can come from our omniscient Father. Sometimes we only imagine God in His glory in heaven, forgetting about the Spirit emanating from Him. Life's challenges are conquered not just by praying to the Father but by accessing the sea of wisdom and strength that is in us and all around us. It is hard for us to realize that we are living in a sea of glory that can do more than we ever imagined. It is important to consider the validating scriptures that support the glorious vision of living in God's light and truth that can help us to be unbreakable and then see what academia has to say that testifies of the truth regarding glory.

We live in two interconnected worlds. One world is what is going on inside of you at this very moment. It is your private internal world of your conscious thinking and feeling. Other people generally do not know all of your thoughts and emotions. Your private world is your illuminating noble spirit, your childlike nature, and your innate sense of character. This is your world that, by being born into mortality with its accompanying veil, has darkened any memories of your pre-earth life.

The other world is your spiritual world of glory. The telestial world of nature can infuse your soul with glory that can come from your environment or ecosystem. It comes from where you live, work, and play. It is the telestial world in which we live. We will learn that you can design an environment that can provide peace, inspiration, and comfort. Not only will we explore the glory of your ecosystem but we will also try to understand the nature of the sea of glory in which we live. This is the glory that comes from the Father, fills the immensity of space, and is within us. Once we have established the nature of that glory from a gospel perspective, then we will try and understand the magnitude of that glory through the eyes of academia. We will see how the glory of God can infuse our souls with power, energy, and healing capacity. We will see that the substance and power of the Father's universe that is all around us and within us validates what young Joseph Smith saw and what he wrote after his vision of the Father and the Son.

Glory from a Gospel Perspective

Perhaps the most beautiful and descriptive scriptural passages that describe the world in which we live is found in the stunning eloquence of Doctrine and Covenants 88:7–13.

> Which truth shineth. This is the light of Christ. As also he is in the sun, and the light of the sun, and the power thereof by which it was made.
>
> As also he is in the moon, and is the light of the moon, and the power thereof by which it was made;
>
> As also the light of the stars, and the power thereof by which they were made;
>
> And the earth also, and the power thereof, even the earth upon which you stand.
>
> And the light which shineth, which giveth you light, is through him who enlighteneth your eyes, which is the same light that quickeneth your understandings;
>
> Which light proceedeth forth from the presence of God to fill the immensity of space—
>
> The light which is in all things, which giveth life to all things, which is the law by which all things are governed, even the power of God who sitteth upon his

> throne, who is in the bosom of eternity, who is in the midst of all things.

Among the many reasons to have a testimony of the Prophet Joseph Smith, these seven verses are enough to humble ourselves and recognize that these had to have come from God. Recent contributions in science validate this amazing scripture that the Prophet received so many years ago. Only in the last few decades have researchers such as Dr. Brian Greene, who wrote the book *The Elegant Universe,* or Dr. Candace Pert, who wrote *Molecules of Emotion,* validate this amazing scripture that the Prophet received so many years ago. Dr. Green's contributions are described later in this chapter.

Let's take a moment to reflect upon what this scripture means and then see how academia validates the beauty and meaning of the scriptures. First let's read a couple confirming scriptures to help us understand the nature of the glory of God.

The essential theme that comes from the gospel as well as the academic world that will run throughout this chapter follows in Doctrine and Covenants 93:23–24, 26, 28–30, 33, and 36.

> Ye were also in the beginning with the Father; that which is Spirit, even the Spirit of truth;
>
> And truth is knowledge of things as they are, and as they were, and as they are to come. . . .
>
> The Spirit of truth is of God. I am the Spirit of truth, and John bore record of me, saying: He received a fulness of truth, yea, even of all truth. . . .
>
> He that keepeth his commandments receiveth truth and light, until he is glorified in truth and knoweth all things.
>
> Man was also in the beginning with God. Intelligence, or the light of truth, was not created or made, neither indeed can be.

> All truth is independent in that sphere in which God has placed it, to act for itself, as all intelligence also; otherwise there is no existence. . . .
>
> For man is spirit. The elements are eternal, and spirit and element, inseparably connected, receive a fulness of joy. . . .
>
> The glory of God is intelligence, or, in other words, light and truth.

Again, in Doctrine and Covenants 84:45 we read:

> For the word of the Lord is truth, and whatsoever is truth is light, and whatsoever is light is Spirit, even the Spirit of Jesus Christ.

For most of us, these scriptures are glorious and enlightening but also a little confusing. We will learn in the next section of this chapter that academia is supporting and clarifying these truths. It seems in these scriptures that the terms *intelligence*, *spirit*, *glory*, *truth*, *light*, *knowledge*, and *power* all seem to be somewhat synonymous—but are they really? Let's try to understand the relationship of these descriptors of glory.

- The basic substance that is the building block of everything in the universe is called an intelligence.
- It is clear then that these building blocks are organized to form spirits. These organized intelligences or intelligence-rich spirits are the essence of everything in the universe including people, animals, the earth, and the stars.
- Intelligences, as the basic building blocks, can shine as they absorb light. As intelligences are exposed to truths, they begin to shine, radiating the Light of Christ.
- The Light of Christ emanates from the presence of God via these luminous intelligences to fill the immensity of space.
- Truths are principles and laws of nature that have always existed and will always exist in the future. These are eternal

laws of science, principles of morality, and the foundational law of progression that will be evident throughout the eternities. As intelligences are exposed to truths they shine even more. The truths become part of the wisdom of the intelligences.

- Knowledge is our quest to understand and apply truths in our own lives, and as we do, those truths shine.
- As we acquire more truth and knowledge of the laws of God, intelligences increase their shine.
- As intelligences shine, the collection of intelligences in our organized spirit also shine and are seen as glory.
- In mortality, our spirits that are composed of countless intelligences act upon truths. As intelligences connect with the truths, they shine more, and our spirits shine more. Our foreordination is to find a pathway in life so we acquire enough intelligences with their accompanying glory to begin to take control over our mortal passions.
- As we continue to harvest glory in the telestial world, it will accumulate enough to be worthy first of a millennial terrestrial world and, ultimately over a thousand years, harvesting more glory to be worthy of a celestial world.
- Since shining intelligences are seen as glory and they are the substance of everything, then the universe is governed upon the laws of glory or light and truth.

We can catch a glimpse of how the Father has His power. With an understanding that intelligences can be illuminated with truth and are manifest as glory, it is easy to see that our spirits recognize the greater glory of another. When Joseph Smith was visited by Moroni, he could see the greater glory that Moroni had through his acquisition of glory during his mortal journey and the glory acquired after his death. Joseph was humbled and felt the truth of Moroni's message and caught the glorious vision of translating the Book of Mormon.

When we hear counsel from a person who is clearly in tune with the Spirit, we sense the glory of the truth and listen and are anxious to obey. Even in the extreme cases, when the intelligence that is part of the makeup of the earth is commanded to do something by someone who has more glory than them, even the elements of nature will obey.

With this understanding, the miracles in the scriptures made sense. When Moses parted the Red Sea, it was because Moses became a pure prism that channeled the glory of God and the respect from the intelligences of the water and compelled them to obey and divide, ignoring the mortal laws of physics. Even more dramatic is the story of Enoch:

> And so great was the faith of Enoch that he led the people of God, and their enemies came to battle against them; and he spake the word of the Lord, and the earth trembled, and the mountains fled, even according to his command; and the rivers of water were turned out of their course; and the roar of the lions was heard out of the wilderness; and all nations feared greatly, so powerful was the word of Enoch, and so great was the power of the language which God had given him. (Moses 7:13)

We can see from a gospel perspective that you have within you organized and glorified intelligences that make up your spirit. Glory varies from person to person and from animal to animal. According to the scriptures, you are walking, living, and breathing in a sea of glory that is amazingly powerful, and we can become more powerful as we humbly seek light and truth in this life.

GLORY FROM AN ACADEMIC PERSPECTIVE

It is interesting to witness the gradual evolution of academic disciplines as they unknowingly begin to embrace gospel principles, yet the principles are disguised in an array of semantic variances. There are many names and views for the boundless energizing glory of God. We know that the Spirit can enliven us to feel, perform, and think better than we do normally. It is almost humorous to witness people disagreeing about the origin and nature of spirit when they are speaking about the same thing.

However, in their study of enlivening energy, these academic and philosophical sources help us to better understand the nature and power of glory. It is important for us in developing an unconquerable resilient spirit that we have within us an abundance of glory from the Father and an awareness of the glory all around us. The solutions to conquer and strive in life challenges is a function of connecting to the unbelievable sea of glory in which we live but cannot see with our mortal eyes. Let's explore the perspectives of the gospel that are enriched by an understanding of some of the perspectives from academia.

Intelligences and Spirit are Real and Omnipresent

Both Eastern medicine and theoretical physics support that idea that intelligence with its accompanying glory is real. Both of these two academic views describe the foundational building blocks of all things as tiny energy packets that are everywhere and in everything. Even these disciplines suggest that we are living in a world of intelligences with glory that is within us and all around us. Let's take a casual look at theoretical physics to help us validate the enlightened revelations from the Prophet Joseph as described earlier.

Theoretical physics is an academic discipline that borders on science and approaches philosophy. There are various descriptions in the literature that describe basic foundational building blocks of everything in the universe. Whether they speak of quarks as the building blocks of organized hadrons or string theory, most of the concepts support the same relationship we just reviewed between intelligences and spirit. The most daring argument is the suggestion that the basis of all life is a one-dimensional energy unit called a string, among other name variations. Strings are mathematically calculated to be a billion, billion times smaller than an atom. With today's limited technology, strings cannot be seen because they are so infinitely small, but mathematically, they do seem to exist. This sounds like intelligences.

Consider this wonderful parallel with the gospel. String theory seems to be the fulfillment of Einstein's dream of uniting all the forces of the universe into one force. These infinitely small strings of energy unify and control the force of nature into one force. Where the force of gravity (attraction of two masses), electromagnetism (electricity and lightning), the strong nuclear force (neutrons and protons hold atoms together), and the weak nuclear force (beta decay turning neutrons into protons) are considered separate, string theory—at least mathematically—combines all the forces of nature into one unifying force. It explains how big things move (general relativity) as well as how little things function (quantum mechanics).

When I read of these recent discoveries, a confirming spirit of truth came over me because it was so clear that if strings are the controlling unifying force in the universe, then string theory has just validated the glory and power of God. The intelligences and glory of God are true and real. Let's explore what academics are saying about these intelligences or in their words, strings.

According to string theory, these little bits of energy activate everything in the universe and control the order in all things. It is difficult not to have images of the fictitious character Yoda in the *Star Wars* movies moving objects using the Force. The common little energy packets are part of us and around us and are the vitalizing force in everything. In theoretical physics, it is nicknamed the "theory of everything."[1] I continue to be thrilled as I hear about these wonderful perspectives in science that validate the nature of intelligences and everything that we believe as per Doctrine and Covenants 88.[2]

These strings energize everything with us and are connected to the strings in the universe in which we live. Everything in the universe is formed by the way these strings vibrate. Strings are just another way to describe the glory of God.

Theoretical physics is one validating perspective of the glory of God, but the time-tested perspective from the Eastern philosophies also helps us confirm that spirit is real. Eastern medicine has practiced energy healing techniques for centuries. Eastern medicine is founded upon the belief that we have energy fields running through our bodies and we also are living in a world of energy. Approximately four hundred years before Christ, a mystic Chinese philosopher named Lao Tzu wrote a book called the *Tao Te Ching*, for which he is considered the founder of Taoism. The Tao means "the way," and Taoism is about following "the way." The way is an energy field called *qi*, the source, pattern, and substance of everything that exists. Taoism suggests that living in harmony with qi or the spirit is the natural way and is simple. *Qi* is literally translated as breath, air, or gas. Qi is experienced as soft vibrations in nature and the universe, which connects people with a soft energy flow. Qi moves everything at the molecular, atomic, and subatomic levels. Taoists practice skills to feel qi, which promotes healing, peace, and other spiritual qualities throughout their bodies.

What is also interesting is that philosophies and cultures across the planet are striving to understand spirit as we do in the gospel. Everyone that is living on the earth had glorious spiritual experiences in the first estate and are longing to feel it in the second estate. Look at other cultures and belief systems, and you will find that most have a concept and word for intelligences or organized intelligences as spirit that help them to feel spirit and glory as we have. In Japan, it is called *ki*, and in India, *prana* or *shakti*. The ancient Egyptians referred to it as *ka*, and the ancient Greeks as *pneuma*. For Native Americans, it is the *Great Spirit*. In Africa, it's known as *ashe*, and in Hawaii as *ha* or *mana*. It is truly amazing that so many cultures believe in the common phenomenon of being in a world full of glory. The belief is common even though we can't see, taste, or hear qi. It is felt in every culture. We can feel blessed that we have a deep understanding of the nature of the glory of God. Try the following activity.

Activity: Walking in the Sea of Glory

> I want you to imagine for a moment that you are walking outside on an invigorating yet comfortable night in a natural setting. Imagine the natural trees and flowers all around you and perhaps a gentle stream babbles a distance away. As you look upward toward the clear and glorious sky, you see the heavens peppered with stars.
>
> You ponder the awe and wonder of this beautiful night. Picture in your mind that the stars begin to shower tiny bits of glory or light, and you watch them gently descend down to earth. You can sense their touch as they gently rain upon you.
>
> As you walk through these little specks of glory, you can feel the wonderful infusions of energy as they gently light on you. Imagine the feelings as these particles of light or glory fall and you feel bits of peace and love come over you. Other specks of light touch your spirit from your noble pre-earth life. The illuminating bits of glory begin to light your whole soul. The spiritual qualities that you need to conquer life challenges begin to shine within you. You feel more courageous. You feel the sea of glory igniting your hope and optimism.

> As you inhale, the specks of glory fill your lungs and then your soul with the love of God, of others and yourself. Imagine breathing in and feeling the glory consume your entire being.

GLORY IS IN YOUR ECOSYSTEM

We have a wonderful opportunity when we are seeking strength to become unconquerable as we face life challenges. We can get wisdom, courage, hope, and peace from the soft vibrations of nature and other sources in the world around us. Remember this basic scripture that tells us of the spirit and glory that are in the world around us.

> And every plant of the field before it was in the earth, and every herb of the field before it grew. For I, the Lord God, created all things, of which I have spoken, spiritually, before they were naturally upon the face of the earth. For I, the Lord God, had not caused it to rain upon the face of the earth. And I, the Lord God, had created all the children of men; and not yet a man to till the ground; for in heaven created I them; and there was not yet flesh upon the earth, neither in the water, neither in the air. (Moses 3:5)

Robin Kimmerer, a botanist and professor of plant ecology, wrote a book entitled *Braiding Sweetgrass: Indigenous Wisdom, Scientific Knowledge, and the Teachings of Plants*, in which she describes how plants communicate with each other and can actually help heal each other. As a Potawatomi scholar, she describes humans as the "younger brothers of creation," which is in harmony with gospel creation stories with Adam and Eve being created after the plants. As we look for energy to become unbreakable, we can seek the spirit from the world around us. As Kimmerer states, we all need to awaken to an ecological consciousness that "all that is green and growing [is] a universe that never stopped speaking to us, even when we forgot how to listen."[3]

In resilience literature, ecological resilience is the experience of feeling an infusion of peace and energy from one's ecosystem, including colors, natural settings, music, smells, pets, and home environments. If you need to feel your resilient spirit and your heart is open to it, it only takes stepping outdoors and smelling flowers and trees to feel infusions of peace and comfort. When listening to a favorite musical piece, your mood can be heightened. When watching a spiritual movie, you will feel the stirring of glory in your soul. When you eat fresh-baked bread or cookies from the oven, the taste may inspire fond memories and glory from childhood.

Your magnificent senses of smelling, hearing, seeing, touching, and tasting are like radars scanning your world for spiritual triggers that will enliven your life situation. We all have the yearning for peace, inspiration, motivation, and energy that emanate from the world around us.

We will describe methods that describe how to access ecological glory in chapter 7. Bookstores and libraries are full of books written about sources of ecological resilience. For example, Dr. Esther Sternberg has written a powerful book entitled *Healing Spaces: The Science of Place and Well-Being*, which goes into great detail into the power of an enriching environment.[4] Ecological sources of strength can come from music, nature, historical sites, plants, pets, aromas, art, movies, and other people, among many. If the light and truth in you yearns for peace, inspiration, motivation, and energy, then it seems wise to design an enriching environment at your home, work, play, and with your transportation. Take time to visit places that have ecological richness including the temples, natural settings, and listening to music that resonates within your spirit. Each person is unique and will resonate to one or more of these ecological sources of spirit as he or she tries to enrich the world that nurtures his or her resilient spirit.

Glory from Universal Resilience

We have already described how intelligences and organized intelligences as spirits give light and life to everyone. Those who continue in obedience to God receive more light, and that light can grow "brighter and brighter until the perfect day" (D&C 50:24; see also Alma 12:9–11, John 8:12). The resilient spirit has the yearning and drive to access and connect to the Father's force, energy, or power that is well beyond normal capacity. When you catch bits of glory, despair melts into hope when you realize that you are sailing life's voyage in a sea of enlightenment, peace, and miracles that lie just beyond the bandwidth of the human conscious mind.

We see numerous examples of heroes in Church and American history who have overcome the odds and left legacies of great accomplishment through power beyond themselves. People report feeling power and energy to deal with life crises in a way they had never experienced previously. We see the energy of fear transformed into the power of courage. We see where initial stressors and changes were used as springboards for growth and harvesting of glory. We see confusion at a time of important decision making evolve into keen discernment and enduring confidence.

We see it in the testimony of William R. Palmer, who described his journey pushing a handcart from Iowa to Utah in 1856. The handcart company left a little late in the season, but the powerful spirit of truth and rightness of the journey that assured him kept him going. During the trip, where he pushed the handcart all way, he suffered greatly. As members of the Church we have heard these amazing stories for many years. Years after Mr. Palmer arrived in Salt Lake, he spoke to a group of listeners who were criticizing the decision to cross the plains so late in the season. The infusion of the glory of God was not to be denied as we read his story.

> I ask you to stop this criticism. You are discussing a matter you know nothing about. Cold historic facts mean nothing here, for they give no proper interpretation of the questions involved. Mistake to send the Handcart Company out so late in the season? Yes. . . . We suffered beyond anything you can imagine and many died of exposure and starvation, but did you ever hear a survivor of that company utter a word of criticism? . . .
>
> I have pulled my handcart when I was so weak and weary from illness and lack of food that I could hardly put one foot ahead of the other. I have looked ahead and seen a patch of sand or a hill slope and I have said, I can go only that far and there I must give up, for I cannot pull the load through it. . . . I have gone on to that sand and when I reached it, the cart began pushing me. I have looked back many times to see who was pushing my cart, but my eyes saw no one. I knew then that the angels of God were there.
>
> Was I sorry that I chose to come by handcart? No. Neither then nor any minute of my life since. The price we paid to become acquainted with God was a privilege to pay, and I am thankful that I was privileged to come in the Martin Handcart Company.[5]

In our journey to become unbreakable, it is important to access this amazing force around us. With the infusion of glory, it helps us to discover jewels of hope in the mire of depression. If we are concerned about what is right or wrong in the gospel, the glory of the spiritual forces will confirm the truth. We see heroes and heroines in sports, business, service, relationships, and in history that have benefited from universal resilience. We knew that God's hands were instrumental for the United States to gain its independence. Historians tell the story of the Continental Army in the beginning weeks of the Revolutionary War where, were it not for universal and ecological interventions, the Americans may have lost that war.

> In the first few days of the American Revolution, George Washington's poorly trained Continental Army of about nine thousand was facing the British army, the most powerful military force in the world at that time. Washington's soldiers found themselves trapped at the end of Long Island with the East River at their backs and thirty thousand disciplined and trained British soldiers at their front. The British had formed a half circle around the Continental Army, which offered no escape.
>
> While the two army encampments prepared for battle, the British commander, William Howe, for some reason chose not to attack for two days. Instead, the British soldiers lay in siege even though a victory was imminent and the American Revolution would have been smothered in the first days of the war. Washington's army tried to prepare for the likely suicidal resistance. As the British prepared to attack the next day, a storm arose, which again delayed the assault on the Continentals. Washington and his officers saw this as a chance to escape. During the storm, the Continental Army made a daring plan to flee. They secured as many small boats as possible. In the dark of night, they secretly began to transport troops across the expansive mile-wide river in order to escape the impending tragedy. All through the night, the boats crossed again and again, evacuating the army across the restless waters of the East River.
>
> As the sun rose the next morning, many troops were still on the island, and it became clear that the army needed at least another three hours before the escape would be complete. As destiny or divine province would have it, the Continental Army's

> escape was protected by a dense fog. Major Benjamin Tallmadge wrote in his journal, "At this time a very dense fog began to rise, and it seemed to settle in a peculiar manner over both encampments. I recollect this peculiar providential occurrence perfectly well; and so very dense was the atmosphere that I could scarcely discern a man at six yards' distance. . . . We tarried until the sun had risen, but the fog remained as dense as ever."[6]
>
> The army was given enough time by the fog to escape and regroup away from enemy lines and later were reinforced to fight the great American Revolution. The United States would not have won the war by all accounts had it not been for the "miracle" of the protective fog. Upon receiving great praise for his leadership in the war, General George Washington wrote, "I was but the humble Agent of favoring Heaven, whose benign interference was so often manifested in our behalf, and to whom the praise of victory alone is due."[7]

The Continental Army's escape was truly God's glory that provided the protective fog. It was God's glory that pushed William Palmer up the slope with his handcart. If we are humble and it is God's will, then His glory will guide us when deciding careers, who to marry, and how to get out of difficult situations. We all long for miracles, and the reality is that the power is there for us.

The Power of Glory

We have talked about living in a sea of glory that is foundational to our religion and is also supported by a number of academic disciplines. We have also described how academics and philosophers speak of a strength beyond normal capacity using a variety of terms yet with common functions. Some of the academic disciplines describe the amazing power of glory using their scientific foundations. Spirit or glory has a number of properties and characteristics that comply with natural laws but in some cases defy normal laws of Newtonian physics. Here are some highlights:

- **Glory carries information:**[8] We can get a hint about the nature of glory from string theory. We learn that when strings (intelligences) collide with each other, they exchange information. The information that one intelligence contains is transmitted to the other so that both intelligences depart enriched. Since the beginning of time, these strings (intelligences) have collided and collected information until they have reached our time. They truly carry the wisdom and knowledge of the ages. The amount of information that these tiny intelligences have is enormous. It has been speculated that if everything that had ever been written since the beginning of time, including every book in every library in the world, could be put on a string (intelligence). Together, that enormous information from the libraries could be put on a massive collection of strings that would fit on a sugar cube. You are living in a world of tiny particles of intelligence. Lynne McTaggart in her book entitled *The Field* states:

  > On our most fundamental level, living things, including human beings, [are] packets of quantum energy constantly exchanging information with this inexhaustible energy sea. . . . All of us connect with each other and the world at the level of the very undercoat of our being.[9]

  It is still amazing to me that the young Prophet Joseph could have envisioned the universe of intelligences only to be validated by academics decades later.

- **Glory has a primary drive to connect and influence:** One of the fascinating qualities of the strings is that they have the drive to connect and organize. That is why as intelligences,

God is able to organize intelligences into spirits. That is why as our spirits take on bodies, we again want to connect with other spirits. The essence of love is the yearning to connect and be with other people as well as to connect with the spirit that comes from rocks, animals, and plants. The connections are evident in animal and human behavior as families, groups, religions, herds, or packs naturally form.

- **Glory has amazing energy:** If you choose to question whether the miracles of the Old Testament really happened or not, then consider how much power glory really has. In string theory, each string (intelligence) only has about a half of a photon's worth of energy. This isn't that much. But remember that a string is a billion, billion times smaller than an atom. To see how much power is at God's disposal to move mountains or part the Red Sea, if we multiply a half photon times a billon billion to calculate the potential energy of something the size of an atom, then suddenly we have an abundance of energy. The Noble Prize winner for Physics Richard Feynman often stated, "The energy in a single cubic meter of space is enough to boil all the oceans of the world."[10] We don't need to doubt that when God sees it in our best interest to have a conquering spirit, there is ample energy to make it happen.
- **Glory can heal:** We have also seen in the scriptures where faith and prayers have resulted in miraculous healings. Glory or light at a soft humble frequency (380 nanometers) actually has a healing capacity. Cells that may have been partially destroyed can be restored to full function when exposed to the soft frequency of glory. Humility and reverent positive thoughts and feelings seem to be healing. In *The Field*, Lynne McTaggart expands on the work of Fritz-Albert Popp, a German theoretical biophysicist who in 1970 discovered that the greatest healing frequency of ultraviolet light was at 380 nanometers. During his research, he came across a phenomenon called "photo repair," in

which you can destroy 99 percent of a cell with UV light, but then repair the damage in a single day by using the same wavelength but at a very weak intensity.[11] In the photo-repair experiments, those weak pulses of 380-nanometer light created a vibration in the field of glory that actually promoted healing.

With priesthood blessings, we have been taught that the priesthood bearer needs to be humble and receptive to the Spirit. The goal of the priesthood bearer is to be as pure as he can so that glory can come from God and through his hands to provide the blessing the recipient desires. The frequency of 380 nanometers is just a little softer than the vibrations the human eye can see or the ear hear. The healing power is truly God's whispering with healing power.

- **Glory has limitless capacity:** The more spirit you have, the greater your capacity to absorb more spirit. This again comes from theoretical physics's string theory and quantum mechanics. This phenomenon opposes what we traditionally think in physics. Let me explain. With traditional thinking, we can think of air being pumped into a container, such as a tire. If we pump air into the tire long enough, the pressure will become so high that we can no longer put any more air into the tire or the tire will explode. But if we are talking about the infusion of light and glory into a container, then the more you put into the container, the more capacity there is. The more glory we have, the greater our capacity to absorb more glory. Succinctly stated, the more glory you seek, are open to, and absorb, the greater your spiritual capacity.

  As we ponder our challenges that have the potential to break us, we know that as resilient spirits we can increase our spiritual coping capacity. The greater our glory, the greater our ability to understanding truth and wisdom. As you can reflect upon the spiritual qualities you really need to be unbreakable, you will again identify peace, courage, hope, happiness, energy, understanding, or enlightenment.

> You can then ask yourself the question, can you ever have enough of the quality? Can you ever have too much peace, courage and happiness? Can you ever have too much glory? Your life of progression toward celestial glory is validated by theoretical physics.

As you face life challenges with a resilient spirit, it is more than your spirit. You are connected to a universe of glory that has amazing power. We need to trust that conquering life's challenges can be accomplished if we can access the glory in the world around us. God's spirit is there. You are walking in that sea of glory. It is also in your ecosystem, and you can experience the infusion of glory from plants, music, pets, and other people. To continue with the story of my accident, let me share with you the experience of going back to church for the first time after months of recovery.

> It was with some difficulty that my wife and children helped me into our family minivan and put the wheelchair into the back as I ventured to attend church for the first time since the accident. We drove the three blocks to the church, and the ritual repeated itself as they helped me out of the car and into my wheelchair.
>
> I rolled into church and was greeted by loving friends who all knew of my accident and welcomed me back to our congregation. I felt a little awkward being the center of so much attention, but I also basked in their warmth and love. I had not been to church for a couple of months.
>
> To me, much of the spirit of attending church comes from the music and messages included in the lyrics from the hymns. I love the powerful, moving pieces as well as the reverent, reflective melodies. After I settled in with my wheelchair alongside the pew where my family was sitting, the opening hymn was announced from the pulpit.

As the introductory organ music touched my ears, I was shocked by my reaction. The music re-created in my mind and heart the wonderful peace I had felt during my coma, and I suddenly felt the magnificence of those endearing memories of warmth and love. The message of the familiar hymn touched my soul. "The Spirit of God" filled my whole being as though it were on fire. I began to weep uncontrollably. I tried to stop crying, but the powerful music kept playing. I'm sure I embarrassed my family, but I could not hold it back. The music inspired me and lifted my spirits!

Notes

1. Brian Greene, *The Elegant Universe: Superstrings, Hidden Dimensions, and the Quest for the Ultimate Theory* (New York: W. W. Norton, 1999), 15.
2. If you are interested, there is a PBS special called *The Elegant Universe* with Brian Greene from Columbia University you can watch that absolutely confirms the awe and wonder of spirit. It can be found on the PBS.org website.
3. Robin Wall Kimmerer, *Braiding Sweetgrass: Indigenous Wisdom, Scientific Knowledge, and the Teachings of Plants* (Minneapolis: Milkweed Editions, 2013), iv, 9.
4. Esther M. Sternberg, *Healing Spaces: The Science of Place and Well-Being* (Cambridge: Harvard University Press, 2009).
5. William Palmer in David O. McKay, "Pioneer Women," *Relief Society Magazine*, January 1948, 8.
6. Benjamin Tallmadge, *Memoir of Colonel Benjamin Tallmadge* (New York: Thomas Holman, 1858), 12–13.
7. George Washington, *George Washington to the Connecticut Legislature, October 17, 1789*, Letter, From Library of Congress, *The George Washington Papers.*
8. Brian Greene, *The Elegant Universe*, directed by Joseph McMaster, David Hickman, and Julia Cort, aired September 28, 2003 (Boston: NOVA, 2003), http://www.pbs.org/wgbh/nova/physics/elegant-universe.html.
9. Lynne McTaggart, *The Field: The Quest for the Secret Force of the Universe* (New York: Harper Perennial, 2008), xxvii–xxviii.
10. Richard P. Feynman, *Six Easy Pieces: The Fundamentals of Physics Explained* (Harmondsworth: Penguin, 1998).
11. Lynne McTaggart, *The Field: The Quest for the Secret Force of the Universe* (New York: Harper Perennial, 2008), 39–40.

5

The Unbreakable Soul

Integration of the Body, Mind, and Spirit

As a teenager growing up near San Diego, I would have church activities at the beach. We would play football, body surf, and cook hot dogs over the open pit fires. In the evenings we would watch amazing sunsets over the vast Pacific Ocean while we sang campfire songs and our youth leaders shared inspirational thoughts. Periodically, the beautiful sunsets would highlight a magnificent schooner with two or three masts with white billowing sails. As these striking ships sailed across the red and orange sunsets, my mind would often drift into childlike fantasies. I would try to imagine what it might be like to be one of the early explorers who dared to leave the safe harbors of Europe and try to cross the Atlantic Ocean in sailing vessels much like the ones I was watching. I imagined the courage it would take to venture into the vast ocean in hopes of discovering land, not knowing for sure if there was land out there or if the ocean suddenly dropped off at the edge of the earth. Week after week these brave souls would sail into the never-ending sea and at the end of each day of sailing finding themselves still navigating toward undiscovered lands. Venturing into this mortal world is much like the brave sailors that crossed the seeming endless horizons of water.

The schooner with its sails seems an appropriate symbol for this chapter that focuses on your unbreakable, or shall we say your unsinkable, soul. To this point in the book, we have been treating your resilient spirit with its yearnings and drives to have an adventurous childlike nature and to live within your energy-conserving moral character. We have talked about your glorious noble spirit that is connected to a universe of divine intelligences and glory. For quick review, we can also see where we are on the resiliency model or plan of salvation model.

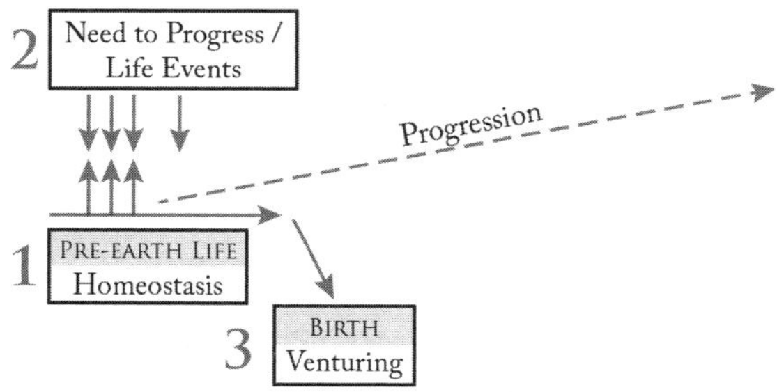

Using the sailing metaphor, we are now ready to move along the plan of salvation model by setting sail into our mortal experience. Your innocent spirit that is endowed with glorified intelligences is now housed in a physical yet vulnerable body. Your mind that was evident in the pre-earth life is still in control even though the memories of the first estate are buried. Elder Merrill Bateman and his wife Marilyn clarified the transition from the first estate to the second estate.

> The earth was created to be a learning laboratory for the body and the spirit. A veil drawn over our minds helps create this new laboratory (see 1 Corinthians 13:12).

> The veil separates us from the Lord, blanks our memory of the spirit world, and causes us to depend more on our own strength in making decisions. Spiritual development occurs when prayer draws us close to God and we choose to be obedient. Part of the earthly challenge is to pierce the veil, even in part, so that we may receive the Lord's guidance.[1]

As an infant you needed nurturing. You needed to be fed, be clothed, and have all your needs taken care of. Your parents would look at you as a baby and could see and feel the radiant sweet innocence of your glorified spirit. Still, in your baby's mind, the main focus in life was on eating, staying warm, being clean, and being loved. You became a living soul, which was the integration and oneness of your mind, your body, and your spirit.

The soul, as recorded in Doctrine and Covenants 88:15, is "the spirit and the body." Elder Russell M. Nelson elaborated when he said, "Spirit and body, when joined together, become a living soul of supernal worth. Indeed, we are children of God—physically and spiritually."[2]

Elder Bateman and his wife added to our understanding of mortality when they stated the following:

> Prior to birth we were spirit children of a Heavenly Father. We had intellect, personality, talents, and agency. As personages of spirit it was possible for us to think and act independently. The scriptures indicate that the faithful spirits, those who accepted and lived the Father's plan, were chosen to be "added upon"; that is, to receive a physical body and to have experiences in a new earthly laboratory. The Lord told Abraham that those "who keep their first estate shall be added upon; . . . and they who keep their second estate [that is, mortality] shall have glory added upon their heads for ever and ever" (Abraham 3:26).[3]

To "be added upon" reflects the challenge of mortality in taking on a body but still progressing through the acquisition of more light, truth, and glory.

The experience of mortality is to harvest more glory to your soul in this second estate through the amazing interdependence and oneness of the mind, the body, and the spirit. From a resiliency model perspective that deals with daily challenges, we are ready to set sail into a new day of challenges, stressors, and opportunities. Your journey through life challenges and mortality is comparable to one of these magnificent schooners.

Your Physical Body as the Structure of the Ship

Your physical body—or temple that houses your spirit—is much like the structure of the ship including the hull, the mast, and the sails. To be able to sail, you need to have the hull be built of a sturdy substance. In the early days of the world explorers, the ships were made with carefully crafted wood. The mast was made of a sturdy pole and the sails crafted from strong cloth to capture the propelling winds. Like the structure of the ship, you too need to have a sturdy body to be unbreakable. You are made of bones, muscles, blood, tendons, organs—all of which are controlled by your brain. If you nurture your body, you will be as unsinkable as possible in normal seas. You will be able to face life challenges with energy and motivation.

We have received guidance as to how to keep our bodies strong through the counsel of prophets. One of the great messages about nurturing the hull of your human ship was written by Elder Russell M. Nelson in October of 1987 in the *New Era*. It would be wise to review that entire article. He speaks of the miracles of human body, highlighting and detailing embryonic development, eyesight, hearing, and the heart pumping two thousand gallons of blood every day. He speaks of the amazing immune systems and the control center in the brain. He states:

> When we understand our nature and our purpose on earth, and that our bodies are physical temples of God, we will realize that it is sacrilege to let anything enter the body that might defile it. It is irreverent to let even the gaze of our precious eyesight or the sensors of our touch or hearing supply the brain with memories that are unclean or unworthy.[4]

To assure that our ship's hull is seaworthy, it is important to take care of this precious creation from God. The Apostle Paul stated in 1 Corinthians 3:16–17:

> Know ye not that ye are the temple of God, and that the Spirit of God dwelleth in you? If any man defile the temple of God, him shall God destroy; for the temple of God is holy, which temple ye are.

You can maximize your physical body if you will take actions to nurture it. Beginning in elementary school, you have learned how to take care of your physical body and how to make it watertight for sailing. You know that exercise will help to fortify your body. You know that eating several servings of vegetables and fruits every day will help to make your hull strong and resist the strong water pressures that can collapse your human ship. You know that you need lean proteins and complex carbohydrates to fortify your hull. You know that you need to rest your body to allow it to regenerate energy and motivation to sail the next day.

We have been taught the Word of Wisdom throughout our lives. The Word of Wisdom is the wisdom of Christ. There are many definitions of the word word but one of the most meaningful is that described in John 1:1.

> In the beginning was the Word, and the Word was with God, and the Word was God.

The Word of Wisdom is the wisdom from the Word or the Savior to help us nurture mind, body, and spirit. The fabric that is the connection between the three dimensions of the soul creates a oneness of spirit. Intelligences and glory are the fabric of the soul that connects us to the Light of Christ. The purpose in life is to harvest glory, and we can do that if we are wise with our agency. If we respond to the wisdom of the Word, then we receive the promises in Doctrine and Covenants 89:18–20:

> And all saints who remember to keep and do these sayings, walking in obedience to the commandments, shall receive health in their navel and marrow to their bones;
>
> And shall find wisdom and great treasures of knowledge, even hidden treasures;
>
> And shall run and not be weary, and shall walk and not faint.

Our physical temples also send us messages as to how to care for the structure of the ship. From chapter 4, remember that we are surrounded in our second estate in a sea of glory, light, and truth. Everything around us and within us is made up of that glory. Part of this glory is the collective wisdom from our first estate, which makes mortality tough because of the veil that hides so many memories of the first estate. Part of our mission in life is to access the glory from the greater wisdom that will help us nurture our bodies.

We need to do all that we can do to take care of our physical bodies and help us to become unbreakable. Our bodies are connected to the glory of God and are constantly sending messages of wisdom to our minds. Some messages are very loud and obvious. For example:

- If you accidently hit your thumb with a hammer, the message is loud and clear—"Stop hitting your thumb!"
- If you are struggling to stay awake to watch the end of a

television show, the loud message is, "Go get some sleep!"

- When you haven't eaten in several hours and your stomach is growling, the loud message is, "Get some food!"
- When you are sneezing and coughing the message is, "You are sick; take care of yourself!"
- When you have pushed yourself physically to extreme fatigue, the message is, "Stop and rest!"

Other messages that come from the subtle glory of our bodies are a little softer but still evident.

- When you have been sitting for a long period, your body will tell you to stretch and move.
- When you have had a complete a meal and are satisfied, your body tells you to stop before you overfill. Many do not listen to this message.
- When your mind is fatigued and no longer functioning optimally in your work or in problem solving, you receive subtle messages to take a break.

Remember that glory with its wisdom comes most often when we are humble and soft. The best messages as to how to fortify our bodies come from our resilient spirit. Our resilient spirit is connected to the wisdom of our intelligences, which are connected to the greater wisdom of our Father in Heaven. The soft messages are soulful messages about eating, sleeping, and being active to help us to be unbreakable. For example, try the following exercise to experience soulful eating. Remember, in this situation, you will try and feel the Spirit to guide you to make good choices.

> In a state of openness and humility coupled with your sense of adventure from your childlike nature, go to a grocery store. Do not have the intent of buying anything until the end of the activity. Wander through the store with what you have learned about nutrition in your life such as eating three or four servings of vegetables and a couple servings of fruit each day. You have learned

> that foods with whole grains are best and lean meats are healthier. As you wander through the produce section, stop and focus on one fruit and vegetable at a time. As you look at the fruit or vegetable, try to sense a resonating feeling. Does the thought of smelling, tasting, or eating that particular fruit or vegetable feel good? Does it feel right? Continue through the store and ponder meats and other groceries. Are there foods that give you bad feelings? As you stand in front of sugared cereals, candy bars, or processed packages, ponder what might be in those boxes. How do you feel?

If you listen to the messages of your body, you will resonate to nutritious food because your body needs that food. If you are low on iron, then you may crave liver, broccoli, squash, or a sirloin steak that is rich with iron. If you are low on vitamin C, then when you see citrus fruits, you will sense an urge to eat those fruits. If your vision centers or immune system is weakened, you may crave a carrot or other source of vitamin A. If you are feeling a little down in the midst of winter, your body will crave being in the sun, which is enriched with vitamin D, and if you can't your body will tell you softly to eat tuna or eggs, or drink vitamin D milk.

Soulful eating generally requires that you eat prudently for a few weeks so that your sugar and caffeine addictions are no longer evident. Then you can ponder foods you would like to eat, and you will see that your diet will improve, as will your energy, because you will be eating those food items that your body needs. Soulful eating is challenging if you have sugar and fat addictions. Addictive cravings for a candy bar or a doughnut are much louder than the soft yearnings for vegetables and fruits. It may be best to do this exercise when you no longer have that addiction.

Unfortunately, too many of us weaken the hull of our ships by not taking care of our bodies. We put holes in our ships by smoking, abusing illicit and prescription drugs, eating fatty foods, and overindulging in sugar foods. We weaken our hulls and our masts when we do not get enough sleep or exercise regularly. To have an unbreakable soul or hull of your ship, we need to listen carefully to the counsel of the prophets and the Word of Wisdom.

The sails on your ship long to be touched by the Spirit from our Father in Heaven. It reaches high to be guided and be propelled through the vast seas. Part of reaching out to the Spirit comes from your innate resilience to become unbreakable. In addition to listening to the intuitive prompts that come from your body as to what to eat, if you with listen to the innate resilient yearnings and drives, you will be able to fortify the structure of your ship even more.

Childlike Resilient Spirit

Your childlike spirit is the energizing force that we focused on in chapter 3. We suggested that becoming as a little child is a yearning to be adventuresome, teachable, and curious as well as the drive to have fun, be creative, laugh, and be spontaneous. Sailing is a childlike adventure. Just by acting upon these resilient yearnings and drives you find yourself healthier.

When you act on your adventuresome childlike spirit, it is likely that the fulfillment of the sense of adventure will result in moving. When you are playful, you are moving. When you are sailing, you are moving. When you are laughing, you experience physical responses to relieve tension, boost your immune system, decrease your stress hormones, increase your immune cells (infection-fighting antibodies), and trigger the release of endorphins (your body's natural feel-good chemicals) better enabling you to conquer life challenges.

Your love of play and fun is an obvious adventure to fulfill the yearnings of the body to move, be strong, and to be in shape. It is fun to go to parks and see adults playing games of softball, football, or tag. One of the best all-around exercise programs would be to follow a child around on a playground for thirty minutes to an hour. Think about it. You would be running from the slides to the swings and active apparatuses on the playground. In the process, you would build your upper-body and leg strength, your aerobic capacity, and your flexibility. Your childlike nature, if you listen to it, will prompt you to move and strengthen your soul.

Young children have the ability to go to sleep when their bodies tell them they need to rest. I remember a humorous event when my granddaughter fell asleep in her car seat with a half-eaten cracker hanging out of her mouth. Children will sleep when it is time, whether a cracker is eaten or not. Adults have the same abilities to sleep when their bodies tell them to, except that their minds are preoccupied with schedules, tasks to be performed, worries, or the need to watch their favorite late-night TV show. You still have the same abilities to fall asleep if you use your mind with its agency to recharge the magic of your childlike spirit.

You can see how you can fulfil your childlike yearnings and at the same time optimize your need for exercise, eating well, and sleeping to fortify your body. To apply these important principles of listening to your childlike yearnings to motivate you, you can use a simple matrix. On one side, consider the yearnings of your childlike nature, and on the other side, place healthy habits that will fortify your body. For example, when you pair adventure with healthy eating, an image can come to mind about the adventure of trying new healthy foods. Perhaps you may adventure into experimenting with food by combining vegetables into a type of stew or soup that you haven't eaten previously. With adventure and aerobic activity, you may imagine yourself hiking and exploring nature. You can continue to do such pairing throughout the boxes in this forced matrix.

CHILDLIKE RESILIENCE	HEALTHY EATING	AEROBIC ACTIVITY	WEIGHT CONTROL	RESTFUL SLEEP
Adventure				
Play/Fun				
Spontaneity				
Creativity				
Curiosity				

One of the great gifts of your childlike mind is your ability to fantasize and escape reality, which you can embrace to help you sleep, for example. Remember that glory is the light of Christ and the power therein can do miracles. Each piece of glory or intelligence will enter your body as you try the following.

> After doing all the chores and preparations you need to do before you go to bed, assure that where you sleep is comfortable (lights, sounds, and surroundings). As you lie down to sleep, begin by breathing diaphragmatically (with your stomach moving, not your chest). Imagine refreshing air flowing into your lungs, and with each exhalation, you feel yourself becoming more relaxed. Do this several times. You can now visualize that the air coming into your lungs, carrying intelligences or little bits of glory. The glory fills your lungs with peace and contentment. With each inhalation the stress and worries of the day leave your body. You feel yourself becoming sleepy. With each inhalation, the bits of intelligences calm you and cause you to become sleepier. With each exhalation, the tension and stress from the day is blown out of your soul. Continue to imagine these little bits of glory as they continue to cause you to become drowsier and drowsier.

NOBLE SPIRIT

If you feel the glory from your first estate in your soul, you will feel your nobility. You will sense a warm spirit to connect with others. Your mind will sense from your foreordination and mission that you need to serve others. You feel the yearning to build your kingdom or queendom by helping, listening, and nurturing. Just by saying the word "helping," suddenly your mind, as the control center, creates ideas and images of shoveling walks after a snowfall for those that can't or walking dogs for members and neighbors that have physical challenges. Your noble spirit begins to urge your mind to volunteer for church assignments to set up chairs or work at a welfare center. Your noble spirit prompts your mind and then your mind acts in a way that nurtures your body and increases your physical activity.

THE MIND AT THE HELM

Your mind is the captain of the ship. The conscious mind controls the actions of the integrated soul. You can adjust the sails to take full advantage of the wind. You can steer the ship in any direction that you want. You have the agency to go off the course, but the spirit in you wants to be in harmony with your foreordination. To do all of that, the captain needs to learn how to sail. Your mind is the learning center and the decision maker as to how to deal with life challenges. With all the influences around you, sailing in mortality comes down to you holding the helm. The helm is the steering mechanism that you control, by which you choose which direction to sail. You have a compass that guides you through life and will help you gather glory.

The scripture and words of the prophets will help keep you on course. As captain of your ship, you can choose to enter waters that could destroy your ship or you can choose to travel wisely. You have the agency to do that. Elder and Sister Bateman stated:

> It is important to understand that the principle of agency is eternal. It operated in premortality, it was preserved in the Fall of Adam, and it will operate after death. Agency is a key to spiritual development. Righteous choices enhance our potential, whereas unwise choices lower the trajectory of our eternal path.[5]

The formula that we have learned to know whether something is true or not comes from the example set by Joseph

Smith when he was translating the Book of Mormon. In Doctrine and Covenants 9:8, we read:

> But, behold, I say unto you, that you must study it out in your mind; then you must ask me if it be right, and if it is right I will cause that your bosom shall burn within you; therefore, you shall feel it is right.

The same formula can be used when you are pondering how to strengthen and fortify your body to be unbreakable. When you think about fitness, nutrition, and techniques to get to sleep, you study it out in your mind. You read reliable literature to guide you. If you are humble and open, the Spirit will "cause that your bosom shall burn within you" and you will feel the truth with its accompanying peace to know how to take care of your body.

If you have difficulty falling asleep, your mind as the control center can study it out and resonate to one of many strategies available to you that will guide you through sleep experiences. The strategies may range from self-hypnosis to nutritional ideas. There are dozens of effective approaches, and you may resonate to a favorite one.

You may, for example, resonate to the idea of creating a mantra, symbol, or phrase for sleep. As you lie in a sleeping position, you can focus on the image of the Savior, a star, a mountain, or a waterfall. You may want to use a traditional mantra and repeat the word *om*. You may try repeating self-hypnotic words in your mind like, "I am sleepy" or "I feel warm and heavy." You may want to sing a comforting hymn or song. Just by reading this example, you may feel that it is a good idea and you will want to try it. Others will think it will not work for them, so they do not resonate. Study and try several approaches, and one will likely feel right for you.

The Power of Sailing

There is much that we can do to get ready to sail as we have discussed. You can fortify your body so that it will be strong in the turbulent sea. You can learn to sail and navigate with your mind. You can assure that your masts are strong and that your sails will not tear. You can stand at the helm forever, but if there is no wind, you will not sail. Sailing is about the glory in the wind. The powerful wind is the spirit and glory of God. The light, truth, and spirit fills our sails and powers us through life's challenges. It is the resilient spirit that keeps us unbreakable. You can reflect upon how magnificent the strength and power of glory that can fill your sails knowing it is the same power that moves mountains and divides the sea. Glory is also grace, which, through the Atonement, is part of the amazing wind that fills your sails. In 2 Nephi 25:23 we read:

> For we labor diligently to write, to persuade our children, and also our brethren, to believe in Christ, and to be reconciled to God; for we know that it is by grace that we are saved, after all we can do.

As captain, you will learn how to guide your whole soul into safe waters while maximizing the strength of the wind around you. With skills, you can maximize the spirit within you on your voyage to harvest glory throughout your lifetime.

Oneness of the Soul

Sometimes it is difficult to imagine that your mind, body, and spirit are all one system. Remember that the whole earth was created spiritually before it was created physically as per Moses 3:5.

> And every plant of the field before it was in the earth, and every herb of the field before it grew. For I, the Lord God, created all things, of which I have spoken, spiritually, before they were naturally upon the face of

> the earth. For I, the Lord God, had not caused it to rain upon the face of the earth. And I, the Lord God, had created all the children of men; and not yet a man to till the ground; for in heaven created I them; and there was not yet flesh upon the earth, neither in the water, neither in the air.

Intelligences and spirits (organized intelligences) are all made of the same glorious substance. We live in a universe of connected intelligences. The reality is that any change in one part of your soul's integrated system affects the other two. The principle of oneness of the soul applies in an energy-producing and motivating sense. Energizing one dimension positively impacts the other.

String theory in physics suggests that communication between strings (or intelligences, in our language) is instant. When one string acquires a bit of wisdom, all of the strings learn it. There is instant communication between the intelligences in your spirit, your body, and your mind as well as the intelligences and glory in the world around you. Your prayers to the Father are instant! Your body, mind, and spirit are intimately connected and communicate constantly. When you receive a spiritual prompting, it enlightens your mind and energizes your body. When your mind gets an "ah ha" moment and you suddenly "get it," it stirs your spirit and again energizes the body. When you exercise to the point of getting the "runner's high," it clears your mental thinking and boosts your spirit. It is interactive and interdependent.

Unfortunately, the principle applies in a negative sense as well. If one dimension of the soul is compromised, it has a tendency to dim the glory from the entire soul. If you violate a gospel principle, it will result in guilt and drain your whole soul of energy. When assuring that you are an unbreakable saint, you will want to nurture each of the dimensions of the soul.

If we again refer to the sailing metaphor, the hull, the mast, and the sails were all created with glory. You as the captain, were created with glory. The world in which you are sailing is a sea of glory. To conquer life challenges, you want to optimize the several energizing points in your body, mind, and spirit. It is all one integrated and interdependent system.

The Soul's Progression during Mortality

Continuing with the sailing metaphor, over time, wood begins to grow old and weaken. All of us, in our senior years, find that our physical bodies are not what they were in our twenties. Physically, the hull of your ship may not be able to withstand huge waves that challenge the integrity of your ship. Still, with memories of numerous sailing adventures and resilient reintegrations over a lifetime, you still have that resilient spirit. You can still bask in the spirit of the winds.

It is interesting that eternal progression is the experience of harvesting glory over your life span, even into your senior years. When you are fulfilling your foreordination by nurturing your spirit to seek glory, you can progress throughout your lifetime. Unfortunately, you will not be able to progress in all dimensions of your mortal life. Physically, the difficult reality is that you will peak at midlife or earlier, and as you enter your later years, your physical body will begin to get slower and become weaker. So physical progression throughout your life is difficult. We can be physically fit to some degree and mentally sharp into our senior years, but mortality was not designed to last for the eternities. We see in the prophets and apostles, men who are physically aging. Many need canes to get around. Still, the power of Spirit that comes from them in their conference addresses is powerful. Yet it is coming from a weakened physical body.

Progression then can be shown in a graph where age is on the bottom of the graph and vitality and spirit are on the side. Physically, we peak in midlife as shown.

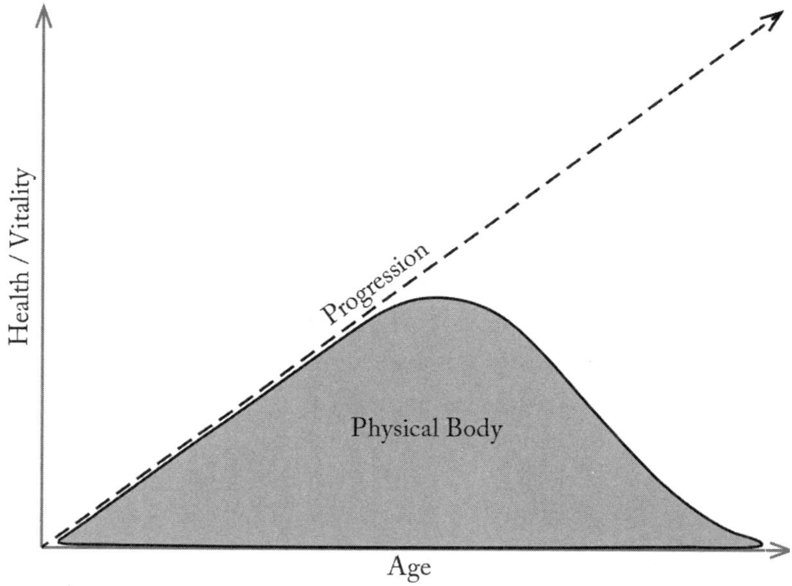

Our minds learn rapidly in the early years, but again, as we age, learning becomes slower. It is difficult to make a case for progression of the mind throughout a mortal journey. This is very apparent in today's world of technology where older people struggle to keep up with the skills of a teenager. So mentally, we also see some decline with age as well, as shown in the graph.

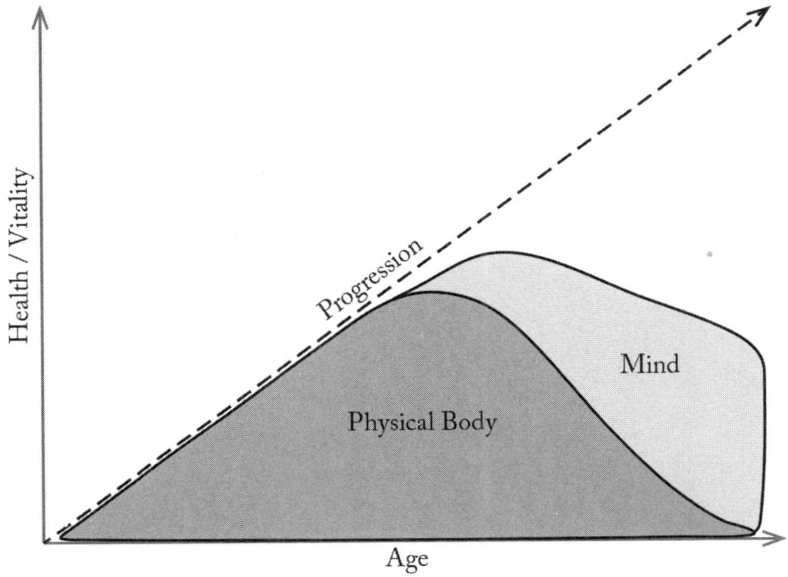

So how do we progress throughout a lifetime? Progression then is accomplished through our spiritual progression. With the qualities of spiritual progression, we can ask ourselves, Can I ever have enough peace? Can I ever have enough love? Can I ever have enough light and truth? Can I ever have enough wisdom? Can I ever have enough happiness? Can I ever have enough integrity? And the most resounding question is, Can I ever have enough glory?

Glory, light, and truth are substances you can harvest throughout your lifetime, regardless of the frailties of the body and the mind in the soul. Hopefully, we have been with seniors who have nurtured their first estate spirit with glorious experiences so that when they are older and in the wake of the decline of their minds and bodies, they still radiate glory, light, and truth. We'll be able to progressively harvest glory in a lifetime of progression.

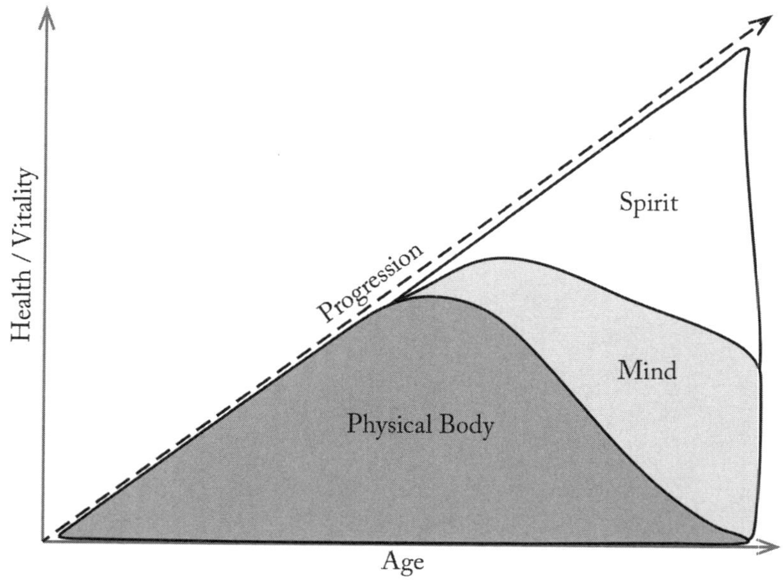

With time, we become unbreakable when we progress spiritually. When we are focusing on harvesting the glory of wisdom, hope, and love we learn to bend but not break.

THE FABRIC OF GLORY THAT INTEGRATES YOUR SOUL

The spiritual first estate experiences and memories are buried in the recesses of your mind, and now, in the mortal condition, you are striving to rediscover your jewels of glory during your lifetime. Remember that you are living in a sea of intelligence, light, truth, and glory. The fabric of intelligences is within you, and all around you is glory. The model to the right attempts to show first, the fabric of intelligences and illuminating glory as represented by dots encompassing the entire figure. The intelligences are within us and all around us and there is constant communication—most of which is beyond our conscious thinking.

Second, we can see your integrated personal spirit consisting of your childlike, noble, and character nature that is living in the sea of glory to which you are connected. We can see the drives of your mortal body and its drives to move, sleep, and eat to maximize physical functioning. Again, the energizing force for your mortal body is glory. We can see the interdependent circle of your mind as the control center with its desire to fulfill the yearnings of your personal spirit as well as discerning what your body needs to functionally optimally. We can see the mind, body, and spirit living in a vibrant ecosystem that includes where we live and the people in our world. Each dimension of the soul or world we live in affects the entire interacting and interdependent fabric of your soul and the glory field in which we live.

THE SEA OF ECOLOGICAL & UNIVERSAL GLORY

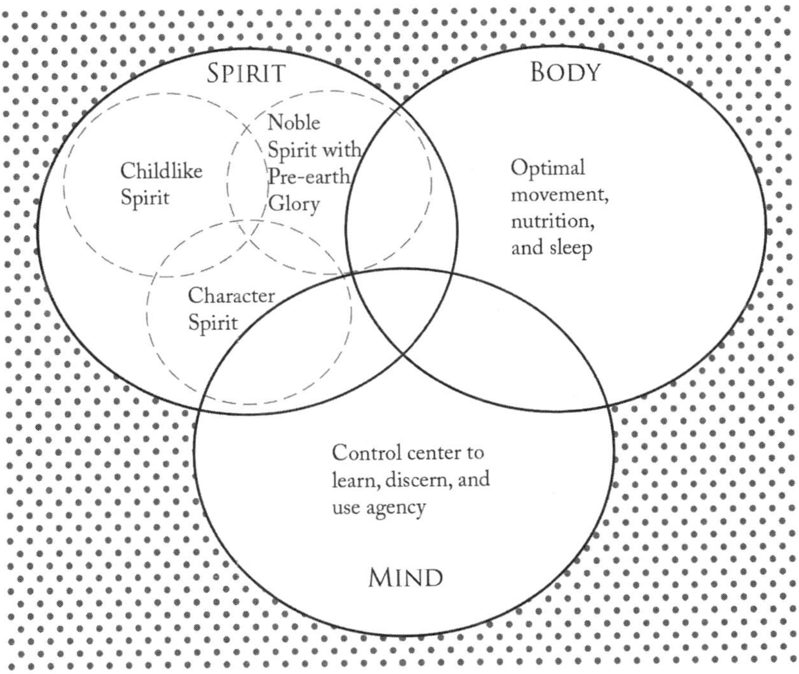

APPRECIATION AND YOUR RESILIENT SOUL

To conclude this chapter, take a moment to appreciate how wonderful your physical state is and how important it is to celebrate mortality. In our pre-earth life, we longed to have a physical experience. Too many people complain that they aren't pretty or handsome enough. They see the negatives as they complain about not being athletic enough or that their skin is too light or too dark. Too many are ungrateful and are not able to celebrate coming to earth to enjoy the long-desired second estate experience. It is good to take a moment and realize how blessed you are to have a physical body.

Your physical senses create stimulating images for you to enjoy while you witness beautiful sunsets, smell wonderful fragrances, taste tantalizing foods, enjoy the tender touch from those you love, and listen to your favorite music. The images create soft gentle vibrations of the Spirit that spread throughout the fabric of your soul. These stimulating images are bits of glory that spread throughout your soul.

Your body's senses can help to enliven your spirit through vibrations that come from your natural world. Too often we drive to work and miss the glory of a beautiful sunrise that touches our minds and spirits. Too often we ignore majestic music because we are buried in thought about our challenges. Too often we eat a delicious meal but don't taste it because our minds are back at work or dealing with home challenges. Too often we embrace our loved ones as a formality and miss the amazing exchange of love between two people. It only takes losing one of our senses to appreciate the great joy that even one sense gives us to inspire us and stimulate resilient spirits.

You should appreciate your body's natural abilities to heal and defend yourself. Just think of the nature of your blood. Right now, in your body, red blood cells are carrying oxygen to all parts of your body to give you the energy to help you be unbreakable. You also have white blood cells that help you fight infection from the thousands of germs you are exposed to on a daily basis. If you are bleeding, tiny non-nuclear cell material called *platelets* are activated by signals released when a blood vessel is damaged. They then release chemicals to call more platelets and other cells, which then cling together, changing shape to form a barricade against the wound to stop the blood from escaping.

Our bodies respond to threats and help us to maximize our defenses. When we are in danger or we perceive that we are in danger, we automatically activate all the systems in the body to prepare to defend ourselves. Our muscles tense to be stronger. Our heart rate and blood pressure increases to ensure enough oxygen reaches our muscles to be able to fight or run away. We breathe faster and harder to ensure our cells have enough oxygen to fuel the energy centers. Numerous energy-producing hormones flood our circulatory system to give us strength beyond our normal capacity. Our pupils dilate to be able to see and respond better.

Too many of us are so focused on our problems that we forget to celebrate our blessings and the positives of life. Many professionals in the academic field of psychology have changed their focus from trying to solve problems to building positive assets and watch the problems fade away. The field of positive psychology, pioneered by Dr. Martin Seligman at Penn State University, asserts that people really want to lead meaningful and fulfilling lives, to cultivate what is best within themselves, and to enhance their experiences of love, work, and play.[6] Again, it is reassuring to see academics striving to adopt the positive spirit of the gospel.

Reflecting again upon the sailing metaphor, you will be able find great joy in facing the choppy and challenging seas in today's world if you nurture your whole soul. You can build a strong vessel and learn to navigate through life's challenging seas. Still, we must always remember that our resilient spirit relies upon the winds of glory to power through even the most difficult challenges.

Notes

1. Merrill J. Bateman and Marilyn S. Bateman, "Mortality and Our Eternal Journey" (Brigham Young University devotional, January 14, 2003), speeches.byu.edu.
2. Russell M. Nelson, "We are Children of God," *Ensign*, November 1998, 86.
3. Merrill J. Bateman and Marilyn S. Bateman, "Mortality and Our Eternal Journey" (Brigham Young University devotional, January 14, 2003), speeches.byu.edu.
4. Russell M. Nelson, "The Magnificence of Man," *New Era*, October 1987, 44.
5. Merrill J. Bateman and Marilyn S. Bateman, "Mortality and Our Eternal Journey" (Brigham Young University devotional, January 14, 2003), speeches.byu.edu.
6. Martin Seligman, "The New Era of Positive Psychology" (presentation, TED2004 conference, Monterey, California, February 25–28, 2004).

6

Readiness to Conquer

Skills for the Resilient Soul

In our pursuit to harvest glory, we can use a variety of skills to prepare ourselves to receive personal revelations. This chapter focuses on the primary emotions and skills (step 4 of the resiliency model) as we continue our resilient journey. Before we jump into the specific skills to become unbreakable, let's review again where we are on the plan of salvation or resiliency model. You can see that when we are disrupted by life events or by choice, we feel the need for God's help to not break. We may be confused and discouraged. When we feel hurt, we long for healing. When we sense a loss, we want to be comforted. When we break a commandment and feel guilt, we ache to be forgiven. When we are afraid, we long for courage. These primary emotions help to ready us to receive inspiration as to how to progress in our situation.

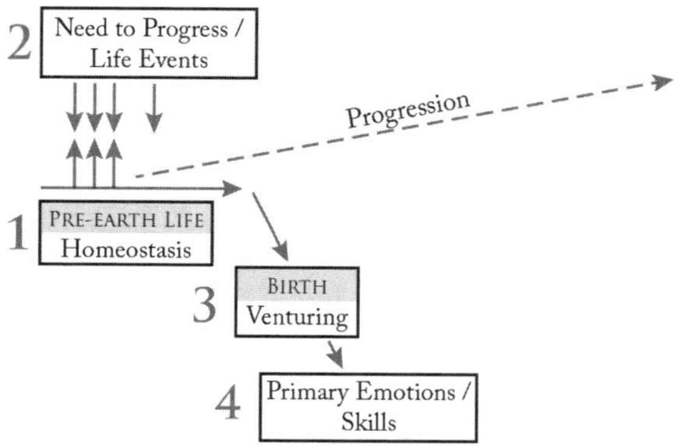

Throughout the history of God's people, there have been remarkable migrations of unbreakable saints. These migrations were instigated when these Saints had a common vision of living in Zion. They envisioned Zion as a place of peace and happiness among all the residents. For example, Moses led the children of Israel out of slavery, seeking Zion. For forty years these nomads continued day after day and week after week with a dream and a vision of a place where they could have refuge. Brigham Young led the pioneer Saints across the plains to enter the Salt Lake Valley, and they called it Zion. It is difficult to imagine the hardships that these early Saints endured, and it warms our souls as we think about their persistence and grit while suffering unimaginable trials. Blood and tears were shed by the traversing Saints looking for Zion. They sought Zion for a number of reasons.

> And that the gathering together upon the land of Zion, and upon her stakes, may be for a defense, and for a refuge from the storm, and from wrath when it shall be poured out without mixture upon the whole earth. (D&C 115:6)

Both groups of God's children sought a refuge without persecutions where they could worship the Lord in harmony with the testimonies and teachings they had received. The vision was to find a place where they could create a Zion after the manner of the original city of Enoch. There, the Lord called Enoch's people *Zion* "because they were of one heart and one mind, and dwelt in righteousness; and there was no poor among them" (Moses 7:18). Having a vision of Zion was so embedded in the hearts and minds of the Saints that they chose to struggle step by step to reach their goal.

One of the ways to help you become an unbreakable saint is to create a personal Zion in your heart and mind. Your Zion is a personal vision and a refuge in your mind to help you thrive and keep from faltering. Proverbs 29:18 indicates the importance of a vision and refuge that states, "Where there is no vision, the people perish." Like the pioneer Saints, when you are feeling vulnerable or weak, facing adversity, or being tempted, your vision of your personal Zion will help you fight through the disruption and continue to progress. Your personal Zion is a place of refuge where you can go to fortify yourself and surface with an unbreakable resilient spirit.

THE VISION OF UNBREAKABLE SAINTS

Like the pioneer Saints who had a vision of what their lives could be in the promised land, you also have a vision. In fact, resilient saints had the same big-picture vision, which is to fulfill their foreordination from the pre-earth life.

Likewise, in your pre-earth life, you had the longing to take on a mortal body and to experience the joys of the soul. You knew that you needed to come to earth on a journey that would allow your spirit to gradually progress until your senior years, when your flesh is weak but your spirit is strong.

Your first estate vision, like everyone else's, was to harvest as much light and truth as you could when you came to live in mortality. You wanted to be found worthy to be resurrected for the entire millennium and ultimately become worthy to inherit the celestial kingdom. You wanted to become aware and access a divine connection through intelligences and glory of God. You wanted to feel joy as you celebrated the adventure, fun, play, laughter, spontaneity, and creativity of your childlike nature. You longed to feel the infusions of glory as you perform acts of altruism to feel your noble worth. You longed for the freedom and innocence of living with character.

When you were born into mortality, the intelligence and glory running through your soul was prompting you to have a vision in harmony with your foreordination. Your vision becomes your purpose and mission as you gradually progress in glory.

Take a moment and simply write a vision or dream statement. Your vision does not change over your lifetime. Your vision is about gathering glory and fulfilling your resilient drives. The following is one example of a vision statement.

> I want to feel enough peace and strength to be connected to the matrix of Father's glory so that I can walk along my foreordained path of light.

The vision is inclusive when you think about what it takes to feel peace and strength. You are feeling peace by living within your character resilience. You are feeling strength because of your childlike energy and the glory that gives you confidence through the nurturing of your entire soul. You know that progression comes by connecting to the matrix of glory around you and within you. You know that your foreordained vision that will optimize your mortal experience comes by following the mark of resonation, truth, and light.

What is your vision? Write it here.

To maximize the vision of your life, you need to be guided by your innate glorious nobility as well as the connecting glory from the world around you. Resilient spirits can learn to enhance their connecting skills to create a personal Zion and refuge to assure their resistance to breaking.

Multidimensional Conquering Goals

Goals, on the other hand, are stepping stones to enhance your vision and harvest glory. You have goals for your body, your mind, and your spirit that are unique to your gifts, skills, and talents. You have the common goals to eat well, exercise, and get adequate sleep but also to have a craft, a profession, and a job in the Church.

You create your own personal Zion with goals that maximize gifts of your soul—mind, body, and spirit. Some resilient saints are good at science, others in music, and some by working with their hands. Some people have gifts of the mind that help them to create amazing electronic apps. The journey to your Zion will be unique and in harmony with your gifts and skills. You will touch lives in and out of the Church through building, teaching, healing, designing gadgets, or whatever your mortal skills are to help make life better for yourself as well as for others. Your personal Zion is a place where you can develop your skills to create a pathway of rightness, peace, and progression as you discover your foreordination.

Skills to Create a Personal Zion

When the pioneers reached Zion, they had to build homes, temples, irrigation canals, and churches to assure their Zion was a refuge. They used saws and axes to cut lumber, horses to help haul the timber to the homes, and hammers to put their homes together. To build your personal Zion, you may also need to use a variety of tools to build a sanctuary where you can go to reinforce the dimensions of your glory-enhancing soul.

A personal Zion is a place in your soul that is nurturing and positive. It is a sanctuary with a collection of memories and reminiscences that enlighten and guide you. It is a collection of experiences that allow you to harvest glory —you can feel the light, truth, and spirit of the memories. Your Zion is a place in your soul where you can go to renew, be fortified, and recharged to thrive through your life challenges.

We will review some of the tools that you can use to build your personal Zion. You can create a refuge in your mind and perhaps even a real safe place where you can retreat to reignite your resilient spirit. The academic field of integrative health and complementary medicine provide guidelines for dozens of techniques and skills that can help you to bounce back from setbacks. The integrative health skills are designed to help you find peace and healing in your personal Zion. Most of us use these techniques to feel better.

> One day I was talking to a colleague at the university who also happens to be a bishop. We were talking about some of the modalities that I would be teaching in my integrative health class when he leaned over and lowered his voice. He told me that when he has difficult challenges to solve in his roles as a bishop, husband, or as a father, he creates a ceremony in his own personal Zion.
>
> He said, "Don't tell anyone, but when I need an answer right away, I turn my home office into a type

> of home temple." After fasting, he would dim the lights and light a scented candle. He then said that he would play a specific progression of music pieces on his stereo. He would start with "A Poor Wayfaring Man of Grief," which put him in a humble state. He would then begin to listen and softly hum "O My Father." During the music, he would imagine meeting the Father and would plead to Him for the answers to his challenges. The aromas from the candle made him think of the celestial kingdom, where he could speak face-to-face with the Father and the Savior.
>
> Another strong member of the Church and former BYU professor told me that when he needed answers to prayers, he would saddle up his horse and go for a ride. He lived in the country where he didn't need to really guide the horse, so he would let her go where she would. He would talk to his horse and then to his Heavenly Father, and it became a three-way conversation.
>
> After asking the Father for guidance and then venting to his horse, he would trust the horse to go where she would go. He trusted that the horse would lead him to signs that would provide comfort or answers to his challenges. Sometimes he would see a plant growing out the crevice of a rock and think of how resilient and hardy that plant was. Sometimes he would come across an ant hill and think of the work ethic and cooperation of the ants. He told me that without fail, as he rode his horse, he could always count on getting answers to his challenges from the symbols he would see along the trail.

Just a quick examination of these two brief descriptions, we see these two resilient saints using aroma therapy, pet therapy, music therapy, and nature therapy. We too can use some of the integrative health skills to have the faith to take leaps into new challenging adventures and also to help when we are approaching the disruptive troughs of confusion, hurt, guilt, fear, or loss.

IMAGERY-ENHANCED PRAYER

Prayer is an obvious skill to help you to connect to the fabric of glory within you and in the universe around you to be able to talk with God while building your personal Zion.

Beginning in the early days of Primary and hopefully in home life, you were taught to pray. Most of you pray seeking answers to your life challenges. Praying with a resilient spirit can deepen the instructions we received in Primary and beyond what is appropriate for formal sacrament meetings. Beyond gentle and peaceful, comforting prayers are communications that beseech the Father in the name of the Son to grace us with bits of glory with accompanying insight, power, or other desired spiritual gifts to help us to cope and conquer life challenges. During times when you may feel that you are on the verge of breaking, the intensity of your prayers naturally increase.

We know that God's Spirit, with all its power and glory, is all around us and within us. Prayer may be more effective if you use multisensory imagery. Simply put, imagery is a skill that we are constantly using every time we daydream, plan, or problem solve. The personal Zion in your imagination is full of multisensory images. In your imagination you can see objects or people, listen to sounds, touch objects or people, taste foods, smell fragrances, sense movements, and imagine emotional feelings. Try adding imagery senses to your prayers. Let's try to enhance the four parts of a prayer as per the instruction we receive in church. We will address the Father, thank Him, ask Him, and close in the name of Jesus Christ. We also need to listen at the end of the prayer.

- **Address Our Father in Heaven:** When you address the Father, you can pause for a moment and create a multisensory scene and imagine Him. A scene in your mind can take you back to your first estate. You can see the angels, hear the singing, and feel the loving warmth that comes from being in the presence of God. As you look at the Father, you can imagine the light and glory coming from Him and encircling and touching you. You feel the love, acceptance, and strength or other qualities you are needing. You can bask in the glory all around you.

- **Thank the Father:** Now you can fall into a world of appreciation. Think of all the blessings you have. Imagine all your loved ones. Imagine how it feels to hug them. See them as clearly as you can as you see their faces, what they might be wearing, and the safe circumstances in which you are meeting them. Imagine the blessings of where you live. Imagine the colors, comforts, and places that make your home pleasant. Ponder how grateful you are for your ability to provide food and necessities. Feel the gratitude of your membership in the Church. Ponder the experiences of going to church and the warm handshakes, inspiring music, the sacrament, and expressions of genuine concern. Imagine these and other positives in your life by imagining the colors, sounds, feelings of embraces, and joys of the world you live in. You can express gratitude for the physical abilities you have and the senses that you cherish to help you enjoy your world.

- **Ask the Father:** As you continue to celebrate basking in the glory of the Father, ponder images of how you can better your life. Imagine your foreordination and purposes. Communicate with the Father about how to touch lives, heal emotional wounds, and find glory in your own life. Try to imagine your future with the Light of Christ within you and how answers to your life challenges will come about. Pray for the qualities of glory that give you understanding, love, courage, peace, and joy. The infusions of these virtues will guide you to know what and how to receive answers. Let the imagery flow with how you will harvest these bits of glory through acts you might take in your imagination.

- **Close in the Name of Jesus Christ:** As you close your prayer, imagine the Savior. Try to imagine the details of the Atonement and His love for you. Feel the glory and grace of the Atonement fill your soul. You can imagine that you are in the presence of the Savior and you feel His glory. You can imagine that amazing feeling of Him holding you as you almost melt in the warmth of the love and light that fills your soul.
- **Open Your Heart and Mind for Answers:** The part of prayer that we often forget is to listen. We will talk about listening and receiving answers in the next chapter. But when you normally say "amen" as a closing and ending, "amen" can now mean "your turn, Father in Heaven." It can be a time of opening your heart and mind in a state of humility, still imagining the Savior, and listening to discern what He is saying.

Activating Glory through Reminiscence

As you build your personal Zion, you can reflect upon a treasury of memories to help you to become unbreakable. As you reflect upon your life, think of experiences from which you have learned and grown. This is the resiliency process in mortality or the big plan of salvation at the eternal level.

You have good memories and others that are not so good. Your personal Zion consists of the positive memories of when you connected to the Father and the Son. It is when you felt the comforting peace of the Spirit. You have memories of when you first felt the gospel was true. You have memories of helping someone and feeling the peace of meaning in life. You have memories of when you met a challenge and conquered problems. This is why journaling is important, because it helps bring to mind fond memories of previous spiritual experiences.

Creating strength to become unbreakable will be found in the remembering and reading your collection of memories and experiences, which is part of your personal Zion. This may be challenging for people who tend to focus on their weaknesses, but upon reflection, you have had more positive and successful memories than bad ones. In your refuge from the world, you go to a safe place in your mind, where your memories are pure of heart and you can rediscover past glories by conquering life's challenges.

Readiness by Two-Way Journaling

Journaling is a method and skill that is encouraged in the Church to write your history, but it is also a good skill to get answers to life challenges. In addition to a treasury of glory from reminiscence, journaling can also be an active method of preparing yourself to receive answers from the Father.

The first phase of two-way journaling is to write to your Father in Heaven about the challenges that are trying to break you. In your imagination, as you bow before the Father, express the concerns and worries of your heart. You need to write long enough so that your total focus is on your writing. You will likely evolve in this first stage from writing about the situation or problem to seeing how it is affecting your life or the lives of others. You will end this first phase with expression of the deep emotions and concerns you have. Open your heart with the feeling of the blessings you have but also the concerns you have. When you finish writing, stop.

The second phase begins by getting a new piece of paper or a new screen on your computer. Now, begin to write on behalf of your Father in Heaven. Your entry starts with "My dearest" and your name. Then write the message from your Father in Heaven. Write how much He loves and cares for you. Keep writing as you imagine His counsel and direction. This technique does take time to get into the right mindset but is very effective in receiving answers to life challenges. The answers to the challenges you are facing may come from Him during your writing.

Another option for this experience is to write a letter to a hero or ancestor whom you admire. It could be someone for whom you have great respect and they perhaps have the qualities you need to be unbreakable. You can write to them and then give that person an opportunity to write back to you through your writing.

Doodling Art for Readiness

Much like journal writing, some people prefer to ponder and think differently through drawing, painting, or just doodling. As you ponder your challenge and need for guidance, think about the situation and accompanying feelings and then begin to draw. Again, to get into a flow state or zone, it may require several minutes. Don't force the drawing; just let it happen. When you write or draw, the process of accessing the wisdom of the Father can come out in figures and images that come from behind the veil in your mind. The greater wisdom as to how to face life challenges with a resilient spirit may be evidenced in your artistic expressions.

For some, performing art is a means for readiness to receive answers through personal inspiration as to how to conquer life challenges. Dancing to meaningful music while pondering solutions can be expressed through your movements. As natural movements result from your ponderings, answers may come through your expressions.

Readiness from Art

If you do not have a real knack for art, then you can enter art galleries and be amazed at the masterpieces that you can see.

You can also look online and see amazing photographs and images. Depending upon the nature of the art, you may feel many of the desired virtues and bits of glory that you desire. Whether the artwork is sculpture, painting, crafts, or photography, you can stand in awe of great works as you feel the infusion of virtues and glory. You can be in awe of the artist's talent or you can find the meaning in the artwork. You can reflect for a moment on a time when you had the opportunity to gaze upon a work of art and felt inspiration though the bits of glory.

READINESS FROM LITERATURE

We continually receive instruction to read the scriptures. Bibliotherapy is about reading literature in your private Zion to help you receive insights and inspiration as to how to deal with life challenges. You can receive insights from various forms of literature including scriptures, Church books, poems, or even children's literature to help you garner strength to become unbreakable. Examples of heroes in literature can often inspire us to follow their examples.

It is important to remember that all the techniques to prepare us to receive answers to our prayers require time. You may receive answers by reading a few verses or you may need to read an entire book. I remember vividly a point on my mission to Brazil when I was truly converted to the gospel.

> I had finally developed some confidence with the Portuguese language after being a junior companion for five months. I was transferred to Santos, Brazil, and got a new junior companion from Idaho. I was excited to be a senior companion and help my new companion get acclimated to his first assignment. We had worked about a month with some success but then found ourselves tracting in an area where the people seemed ready to receive us—not to listen but to challenge us.

In this particular neighborhood, most of the people we met seemed to belong to the same protestant congregation. Each family had a routine of inviting us in and then attacking the two young Mormon missionaries. They threw question after question at us that we really could not answer. After a couple of weeks of this, I began to question my own testimony.

I had grown up in an amazing youth church group with a bishop who made us feel like the most important people in the ward. We had spontaneous testimony meetings after church softball games and clung to each other socially since there were so few LDS members at our schools. I had a coat-of-armor testimony that was created by being around great parents, leaders, and peers. Now I was alone with a new companion who was marginally prepared in the gospel, and I was feeling my coat of armor wear away. I began to question the restoration of the Church. I began to question if the Savior was anyone more than a great teacher.

Finally I asked my companion, "Elder, are you ready to teach the lessons yet?" He sheepishly replied in the negative. I said, "I want you to spend this week studying and learning those lessons." Although we went through our normal routines, I spent a lot of time reading, and my companion focused on studying his lessons. I prayed harder than I ever had to my Father in Heaven to let me know if all that we are teaching was really true. I determined that I'd better start with a testimony of the Savior. I pulled out the book *Jesus the Christ* by James E. Talmage and started reading it for the first time. I read most of the day and well into the night. After several days I finished reading this inspiring book at about three o'clock in the morning.

As I closed the book, I just sat and pondered for several minutes before it began. I began to feel a

> warmth and peace as though I was in a soft blanket. I began to feel my senses come alive, and I started feeling the soft tingling confirming messages all throughout my body. The magic of the Spirit enlivened my soul, and I wept uncontrollably as the bits of glory and spirit took over my whole soul. I didn't even try to sleep, nor did I want to sleep that night. I was so relieved and excited to have a testimony that came from within me and not from others. I cherished every truth-confirming moment. I finally knew what it meant to have a testimony and it came through reading that treasured book. When six o'clock came, I told my companion that he was ready and that we were going to rock and roll. Interestingly, that very morning we were led to some amazing people who were hungry for the gospel.

I only tell this story to describe how reading spiritual literature can create a readiness for you to receive infusions of spirit.

Cinema Readiness

There are dozens of Church-produced movies that are inspiring and will add to your sanctuary of tools to ready yourself to receive answers to life challenges. Going to LDS.org will lead you to inspiring movies and clips that can help ready you to receive personal revelations.

There are also popular films that can ready you to thrive in the face of adversity. Pondering family issues, you may want to watch the classics *The Sound of Music* or *It's a Wonderful Life*. Perhaps you can focus on inspiration by watching *Field of Dreams*. Most of us like to go to movies. Sometimes we go to comedies and identify with the humor and fun the actors are exemplifying and then find humor in our life challenges. Sometimes we go to adventure movies that quicken the spirit of adventure and courage within us to be unbreakable. Sometimes we watch tender romantic movies that help us to remember to be a better spouse. Sometimes we go to meaningful dramas that may trigger the spiritual nature within us.

Now I am taking a chance here, but other adventure stories that show courage and persistence may motivate you in movies such as *Rocky* or *Patton*. I am sure that I am not appealing to everyone by my classic selections, but the point is that you can walk out of a good movie and feel more motivated, tender, or whatever quality you are hoping for to be able to receive inspiration.

So when you are feeling vulnerable, you can enjoy the infusion of glory that will come to your soul. Sometimes it may take seeing the entire movie again and sometimes it only takes a four- to five-minute clip of the impactful parts of the movie.

TAI CHI OR CHI GONG

Taking readiness in another way is to consider the foundational concepts in Eastern medicine. The concept of qi or chi is a phenomenon that is defined as vital energy. According to the Eastern philosophies, qi is in everything and connects to everything. The vital energy of qi is around us and within us. It sounds much like glory, light, and truth. There is much to learn from tai chi regarding the importance of opposing forces for progression—the concepts of yin and yang.

Let me suggest that you access an instructional video of someone doing tai chi or chi gong on the internet. As the instructor guides you through movements to move the qi throughout your body, simply substitute the concept of qi with glory, intelligence, or spirit. You can imagine these intelligences that are bits of glory running through your entire body. As you make the move according to the instructions given in the video, you can feel the Spirit run through your meridians. You can find the peace or courage or whatever quality you need to be unbreakable as you feel the flow of glory in your system—like qi.

If you explore further some of the concepts of tai chi, you learn too that there are seven chakras or wheeling points of energy in the body. You can study these points as well, and when you need the Spirit more than other times, you can press on these points and feel the increase intelligences helping you.

Readiness through Meditation

Meditation is a mind-body skill that focuses on the present moment and living life fully in the here and now. Optimally, meditation allows you to create a calm state of mind and to keep an open mind and heart. In meditation you try to be in the present moment and not worry about the past nor the future. Your Zion is the present.

Most people struggle to empty their minds; rather, they have extraneous thoughts crash into the empty space. Meditation practitioners have developed other ways to meditate that are somewhat easier to master that we can apply when readying ourselves to receive personal revelations. Many practitioners advocate the use of mantras (where the word *mantra* refers to an anchor word that has personal meaning to you) or concentrating on one thing, such as breath, to aid in spiritual development or relaxation. In contemplative forms of meditation, a mantra is a meaningful word, phrase, chant, or image that is continually repeated in your mind until it is felt throughout your whole soul. Here are examples that will help you be ready for personal revelations.

- Repeat the word or mantra *love* in your mind over and over. Love means connections, and you feel connected to your glorious pre-earth spirit. You can repeat the mantra and feel the glory fill your soul. Continuing to repeat the word *love*, you will feel connected to others you love—family, friends, pets, and your living space. You will feel connected to your

Heavenly Father and feel His strength as you repeat the word *love* over and over.

- If you need other spiritual traits to add more to your personal Zion, you can create a mantra to repeat that will fill your soul with that trait. Repeating words that are meaningful to you such as *submissiveness*, *humility*, *courage*, or *spirit* may help you become spiritually ready.
- Readiness for personal revelation may be reached by paying attention to an object that has meaning for you. The object can represent your source of enlightenment. Perhaps you can light a candle and focus on the flame. You can imagine that it is the Light of Christ and the warmth is His Spirit. Use other images that will ready you to receive insights. Perhaps an image of a temple, the Savior, or a favorite scriptural hero. The intent is to focus on the image and it will prepare you to be ready for insights to conquer life challenges.

Readiness through Aromas

Aroma readiness is the practice of using natural oils extracted from flowers, bark, stems, leaves, roots, or other parts of a plant to enhance psychological and physical well-being. I mentioned earlier about the bishop who would use the aroma from scented candles to put him in the right humble state of mind to resolve the challenges he was facing. When you are ready for enlightenment or to discover the resilient saint within you, you could create particular smells to help you acquire the desired state in your personal Zion. The smell is the trigger to get you prepared. You can create your own positive experience with aromas. You may want to choose a smell that helps you to be spiritual or more humble. You may want to create a smell that you associate with being more creative and energetic. It could come from a candle or particular cologne or perfume. You may associate the smells of baking bread or cooking breakfast as a trigger to create feelings of family connections.

Readiness with Water

Water is an amazing source of energy and motivation in becoming unbreakable. In the womb before you were born, you were nurtured in a watery environment. Even now, you can be invigorated by jumping into a cool water, or you can relax by laying in a warm bath. You can laugh and play, evoking your childlike spirit by getting into a friendly water fight with hoses, running through sprinklers, getting into a squirt-gun war, or finding yourself launching water balloons. You can bond and connect with others chatting in the relaxing environment of a hot tub. You can ponder meaning and purpose sitting with your feet dangling in a lake or stream or sitting on a beach overlooking the ocean.

Water is used in the treatment of numerous physical health problems. Water can also be used to promote your spiritual state. A Bavarian monk, Father Sebastian Kneipp, helped popularize the therapeutic use of water in the nineteenth century. Father Kneipp preached that nature had endowed man with everything he needed for a happy, healthy, and fulfilled life. He bathed in the pure streams of his native Bavaria and developed a science of water therapy. After curing himself of a serious case of tuberculosis—considered incurable at that time—he began intensive work on the healing powers of water. People practice many dozens of methods of applying Kneipp hydrotherapy, including baths, saunas, wraps, and packs. We have learned that warm water relaxes and soothes the body. It reduces stress, which helps with sleep and also relieves sore muscles. It also helps to ready you for receiving insights and inspiration as to how to fortify your resilient spirit.

In your personal Zion, you can soak in a bath or swim in warm water to relax you and help you to ponder life's options. If you need energy and power, then cold water will stimulate and invigorate you to have energy to conquer your life challenges. Whether it be in the ocean, lakes, bathtubs, hot tubs, or swimming pools, this may be a place that distracts you from cognitive functions and readies you for spiritual prompts and messages.

HISTORICAL SITE READINESS

One of the most inspiring, reflective, and appreciative experiences is to visit sites where significant historical events have taken place in preparation to harvest bits of glory. Prior to visiting the site, it is best to review the story about the people, their courage, their nobility, and what makes selected sites special and therefore ready to quicken your soul.

> When I was a twelve-year-old boy, my family took a cross-country vacation from San Diego to Maine to visit my father's childhood home. Although we visited many places along the way, two of the most impressionable stops were our visits to the Sacred Grove and to Gettysburg, Pennsylvania.
>
> I knew the Joseph Smith story. I loved the hymn "Joseph Smith's First Prayer." As we walked into the grove, I realized it wasn't a grove but a forest. I began to wonder where the Father and the Son actually visited the Prophet. My whole family became very quiet and reverent, and all six of us could feel that something special had happened there. I almost felt that I should take my shoes off in reverence and respect. If you have the opportunity to visit sites where God's spirit and blessings were bestowed on someone or a group of people, you can feel the spirit of that event if you are prepared.
>
> We then visited Gettysburg. The park ranger described the great Civil War battle that occurred at the site and shared with great detail the bravery and courage of thousands of soldiers that died for their cause. I was in awe. I stood at the top of Cemetery Ridge and heard the ranger describe the

> Confederate charge. "During the afternoon of July 3, 1863, the Confederate infantry attacked the Union center on Cemetery Ridge. Pickett's Charge momentarily pierced the Union line, but the infantry was driven back with severe casualties. The next few days saw General Lee retreat and his train of wounded stretched more than fourteen miles."
>
> Once again, I was struck with the spirit of the ground I was walking on. I tried to imagine the bravery and loyalty on both sides of the Civil War. I thought about the feelings and emotions that were in the minds of these brave soldiers who marched in Napoleonic combat lines, shoulder to shoulder, into a hail of rifle bullets, cannon fire, and residual smoke. Even as a twelve-year-old, the powerful spirit of honor, commitment, and sacrifice for a cause resonated to my soul. I have the spirit of Gettysburg in my personal Zion to ready myself to have courage to do what I have to do for a cause.

You may want to take the opportunity to think about opportunities that you have had to visit historical sites. Perhaps you have visited the Liberty Jail and have felt the sacredness and the reverence knowing that cherished revelations were received there. You can record those memories and store them in your personal Zion.

Music Readiness

Although there are many other forms of therapies that can prepare you to receive answers to life challenges, we will conclude with listening to music that resonates with you and conjures numerous thought and images. When trying to prepare yourself and get into a humble state of your soul, you may listen to or sing "How Great the Wisdom and the Love." If you need energy to be unbreakable, then you may want to listen or sing music such as "Called to Serve," "We Are All

Enlisted," or "Onward, Christian Soldiers." If you are struggling in your heart and mind to remain faithful in the gospel, you may want to listen to or sing "True to the Faith" or "How Gentle God's Commands."

Secular music can also be helpful in putting you in desired moods. In times of political questioning and needing to feel honor, loyalty, and the spirit of patriotism, you can listen to the "Battle Hymn of the Republic," "American the Beautiful," or even "The Marine's Hymn." If you need to get into a childlike mood, the theme of *Sesame Street* may put you there.

You can customize your day and put yourself in moods that will give you the power and qualities that will help you to be in the right spirit to be unbreakable in a day. The approach is to take time, select the appropriate pondering music, and allow yourself to be guided, inspired, and strengthened by it.

All of these integrative health and complementary medicine strategies can help ready you to receive answers to life challenges. Resilient saints can learn these and other wonderful skills to better prepare themselves for the infusion of glory that provides discernment, direction, and guidance.

7

Resonation and Quickening

The Infusion of Glory

In his book entitled *The Elegant Universe*, Dr. Brian Greene presented string theory as the "the theory of everything." We referenced string theory in chapter 4 when we were describing the nature of glory. In this chapter we will consider what we might call in the Church as the "the glory in everything." All your dreams and the solutions to all of your problems come down to the "one thing," which is described in essence in Doctrine and Covenants 112:10.

> Be thou humble; and the Lord thy God shall lead thee by the hand, and give thee answers to thy prayers.

In every decision, every challenge, and every problem, the "one thing" is that whatever we think or do can be led by God's hand. He leads us with a trail of glory. In the previous chapter, we described several ways to enhance prayer and to use some integrative modalities to help you to be humble. Now we need to know how the Lord will lead us by the hand and give us answers to our prayers. We often talk about prayers, but perhaps we don't talk enough about the experience or manners of receiving answers to prayers. How do we know if the answers that come to us are from God or from our own desires? This chapter is about the "one thing" or "the glory in everything." As you go through your entire life, the only important thing that you need to experience is that "God shall lead thee by the hand, and give thee answers to thy prayers." Several experiences will be described in this chapter that will allow you to follow a conquering path of glory.

Before we move forward, let's review again where we are on the mini plan of salvation or resiliency model. After preparing ourselves to receive personal revelations, we can see that in box 5, we actually do receive personal infusions of glory. In resiliency literature, the concept is called resonation and quickening. From the perspective of the plan of salvation, personal revelation is the experience of progressing line upon line and receiving glory bit by bit. It is the experience of receiving glory, light, or truth as it pertains to your life experiences and challenges. It is the applied theology of everything.

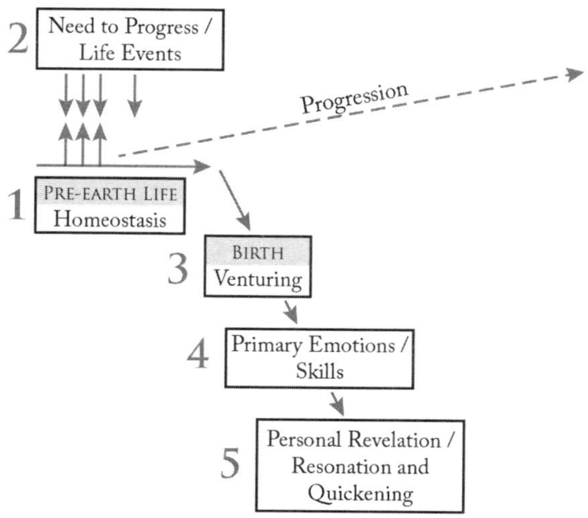

When teaching my resiliency classes at the university, it is inappropriate for me to talk about personal revelations from God. Instead, our discussions revolve about the concepts of resonation and quickening. To start the discussion, I will sometimes show a short clip from popular movies that portray personal revelations.

For example, in the treasured Disney classic movie *The Lion King*, we see a beautiful portrayal of personal revelation within the resiliency process and the plan of salvation. Born into nobility (as you are) the young lion cub, Simba, is the heir apparent to become the king of the lion pride when he becomes older. A major disruption occurs when Simba feels responsible for the death of his father, and the noble young cub runs away from his family and friends. Far away he finds a couple of new friends and begins to live a life of *Hakuna Matata,* which means, according to the joyful song, "no worries for the rest of your days—It's our problem-free philosophy." Rather than finding a way to grow through the tragedy of his father's death, Simba settles for a comfort zone of just eating and playing with friends while essentially burying his nobility. With time, a wise mentor in the form of a baboon named Rafiki guides Simba to look deeply into a pool of water. In the water, as an ecological resilience readiness skill, Rafiki encourages Simba to "look harder." Looking deeper into the water, Simba has a vision of his father who says to him, "Look inside yourself, Simba. You are more than what you have become. . . . You are my son and the one true king." Simba, with that powerful quickening moment, returns back to the pride and fights his way back to become the "one true king."[1]

So many of us need wake up calls to make sure that we are not living life day to day without recognizing that we "are more than what we have become." We let our challenges become our focus and our life becomes a daily fight to just putting out fires and wishing for a "Hakuna Matata" life while ignoring our spiritual drives for progression.

We should all strive for Simba moments, which is to receive personal revelations. We read in Matthew 4:4 that there is more in life that just dealing with daily hassles but that we need to embrace "the one thing."

> But he answered and said, It is written, Man shall not live by bread alone, but by every word that proceedeth out of the mouth of God.

Personal revelations are experiences that come with varying levels of intensity and power. The range of knowing the truth in all things or recognizing words out of the mouth of God range from soft feelings of peace to apparitions from the Savior or angels. In each case, we know that personal revelations come through the gift of the Holy Ghost. In Moroni 10:5, we read that "by the power of the Holy Ghost ye may know the truth of all things."

It is clear that to become an unbreakable saint, we need the guidance, direction, and confirmation by the Holy Ghost. You can be in the depths of problems and on the verge of breaking but then be restored with a personal revelation infused with glory.

Elder Dallin H. Oaks, among others, has given wonderful guiding talks about the experience of personal revelation. At a Brigham Young University devotional address, Elder Oaks spoke of eight purposes of revelation: to affirm a testimony, to prophesy, to give comfort, to uplift, to inform, to restrain us from doing something, to confirm a particular course of action, and to impel a person to action.[2] All of these purposes of revelation help us to be resilient saints and conquer life challenges.

In this chapter, we will explore the range and nature of the personal revelation experience. Some guidelines will be provided to help you discern which moments of enlightenment come with the blessing of the Holy Ghost or whether ideas jump into your mind that are devoid of glory. We will review the timing of personal revelation. We will also speak of personal revelation in light of spiritual gifts.

The Nature and Range of Personal Revelations

In the scriptures and in talks by general authorities, we see a wide array of descriptions of personal revelation experiences that help us to be unbreakable. On one end of the continuum, we read of the actual visitations from the Father and the Son to give clear directions for the Church, such as the visitations to the Prophet Joseph. On the other end of the continuum, many of us feel a sense of a soft gentle assurance that we are on a path in life that is in harmony with our foreordination.

Light and truth come to us with varying degrees of intensity through the fabric of intelligences and glory in which we live and all are accompanied by the confirmation of the Spirit of the Holy Ghost. Throughout this book, I have attempted to integrate resiliency literature to help us understand gospel principles. In this section, again, I describe several experiences of personal revelation that come from both the gospel and the academic field of resiliency.

We will not address the rare and very intense personal revelation experiences. These amazing experiences are reported by the prophets as apparitions from the Father and the Savior. We have read in the scriptures of resurrected beings visiting chosen souls with news of glorious and significant events. Infusions of glory of this magnitude come to a selected few such as Mary, Moses, and Joseph Smith. Most of us do not have sensory visions that we actually see with our quickened eyes.

The focus of this chapter is to consider the more subtle forms of personal revelations, but these wonderful experiences are still glorious and impactful to provide direction and power to conquer life challenges. A review of the scriptures as well as the resiliency literature reveals a number of terms that describe various degrees of personal revelation. In addition to visitations from the Father, the Son, and angels, we read of the more common forms of personal revelations. Here is a list of phrases, terms, or concepts that describe the experience of receiving bits of glory:

1. Guidance by the Holy Ghost
2. Quickening with a sudden burst of directional and energizing glory
3. Awakening one's soul to action
4. A vision of one's direction and future
5. A dream with meaning and direction
6. Waking visions ("The veil was taken from our minds, and eyes of our understanding were opened" [D&C 110:1].)
7. Bursts of joy with accompanied energy
8. Direction to the mind and heart—a voice that you feel rather than hear
9. A voice in your mind—Socrates often spoke about his voice he called his Daimon or inner guide.
10. Intuition and gut feelings
11. Sudden enlightenment or inspiration with new ideas
12. Gestalts—when all the pieces of your life challenges or chaos come together in a simplified solution
13. Epiphanies—"Ah ha" moments or the eureka effect
14. Recurring thoughts with spirit
15. Synchronicity—when things or people seem to enter your life with perfect timing
16. Hunches
17. Resonating to performances and music that have applications to life
18. Resonation to thoughts, feelings, confirming actions, or thoughts
19. Flow—Mihaly Csíkszentmihályi describes being in a zone or fully immersed in an experience.[3]
20. Peace and gentle assurances regarding truths and being on the right path

With these descriptions of how we receive personal revelations, it is clear that we can receive specific instructions. In Isaiah 30:21, we read:

> And thine ears shall hear a word behind thee, saying, This is the way, walk ye in it, when ye turn to the right hand, and when ye turn to the left.

We as unbreakable saints need to rely on the different forms of hearing the Word. Let's explore some of these modes of personal revelation in more detail.

Spiritual Quickening

Quickening, when referring to pregnancy, is the moment when the mother feels the baby move for the first time. It is a thrilling moment when the mother knows that the baby is alive, and it enlivens her entire soul.

Quickening in resiliency literature is a moment of inspiration that also makes a person come alive. You celebrate the infusion of enlivening intelligences and glory that give you direction, energy, and power. Quickening is felt as bursts of joy. Joy is the jolting emotion that vibrates the spirit and energizes the mind and the body. When quickening is experienced with soul-shaking infusions of glory, you will feel a peak experience of well-being, success, bliss, or exultation. Let me restate, the quickening is a tangible feeling of a glory-filled vibration.

A spiritual experience in a gospel perspective is an enthralling experience where you find yourself engulfed in the matrix of God's glory. You may experience this when listening to a talk from a Church leader. Each word that the leader says quickens or softly vibrates your entire soul, and you experience infusions of glory with every word. Perhaps you are praying and you find yourself captivated with a burning in your bosom, catching a vision or image that you are in the presence of glory. It is a moment when bits of glory and intelligence enliven, inspire, and help you to receive personal revelation. These are times of "conversions" or "rebirths" to follow your personal path of progression.

In the scriptures, we read of quickening that has varying intensity. In preparation for being in the presence of God, we need to be quickened to a complete state of oneness with the Spirit.

> For no man has seen God at any time in the flesh, except quickened by the Spirit of God. (D&C 67:11)

The quickening that will be discussed in this portion of this chapter is more for our personal enrichment.

> And the light which shineth, which giveth you light, is through him who enlighteneth your eyes, which is the same light that quickeneth your understandings. (D&C 88:11)

Perhaps the most important quickening experience is when you are off your foreordained path of glory. The quickening will create moments of guidance to redirect you to your proper course in life. Additionally, if you need a boost to strengthen your testimony, quickening will fill and vibrate your soul with light and truth. If you need answers to life challenges, quickening will provide solutions. If you are fatigued, quickening can give you energy to comply with God's will. If you are unsure, quickening will give you a burst of confidence. If you are confused, a quickening moment will give you direction. If you are discouraged, quickening will give you energy. If you are associating with a person you shouldn't, quickening will tell you to end the relationship. Quickening is the moment when the Holy Ghost speaks to you and you understand it clearly.

Assuming you are practicing one or more of the readiness skills described in the previous chapter, you can have the experience of quickening. Using a sailing metaphor, there are moments when you may need to adjust your course. Quickening is the infusion of what you need to do to adjust your sails and reassume a better route to fulfill your progressive path of glory. On the extreme end, it may require turning your ship in another direction to avoid a tempestuous storm.

DREAMS

We all dream when we are sleeping. Some people remember their dreams and others do not. Some dreams don't make sense and others have profound meaning. Lehi's dream was powerful enough to motivate him and his family to leave their home and possessions to travel to parts unknown to them. Other people dream and get ideas as to how to improve their life. When you realize that dreams come from your unconscious mind, which houses the memories of your glorious life in the first estate, you may want to pay more attention to the dreams.

Psychologists have varying opinions about the value of dreams. Some suggest that they are merely our minds sorting through the barrage of stimuli that they receive each day from our different senses. Dreaming, then, is the process of forgetting unimportant memories and storing more important information. The forgetting and throwing out dream images is a sorting process, which may combine together to result in strange and exciting dreams.

Other academics suggest that dreams can have great meaning in your life and may represent what you need to do better in following your foreordination. If you wake from a dream with thoughts and feelings that have implications and meaning about how you can progress, then you will want to consider it a personal revelation if accompanied with resonation.

Some dreams may be symbolic. Carl Jung felt that dreams originated from the collective unconscious mind where the wisdom of the ages resides. The thoughts and feelings from ancestors and great souls might be making suggestions to you about directions and solutions. Jung suggested that dreams may be prompted from the identities of ancestors and heroes (Jung called them "archetypes") housed within our conscious and unconscious minds and we can be receptive to their wisdom.[4]

To simplify, dreams can be a quickening experience that will give you directions in your life. They may also be meaningless. Let me make two suggestions.

First, if your dreams are easily forgotten or seem random, then don't worry or think about them.

Second, if your dream is accompanied by a feeling of resonating glory and that there might be meaning, then ponder it. If it is clear that the dream can correct a course in life, then you should consider acting upon the quickening moment. If it is about a person you haven't seen in a while, then you may consider contacting that person.

Pondering may bring epiphanies for thoughts and actions as it pertains to career choices, who to marry, how to care for children, or how to better fulfill your calling. Dreams can prompt new identities that have more courage, have more compassion, or are more spiritual. You may see a hero in your dream, and it could be the Spirit prompting you to acquire the qualities of that hero.

Burning of the Bosom

When the Prophet Joseph was translating the Book of Mormon, he described how the truthfulness of his writing was confirmed.

> But, behold, I say unto you, that you must study it out in your mind; then you must ask me if it be right, and if it is right I will cause that your bosom shall burn within you; therefore, you shall feel that it is right. (D&C 9:8)

To have the truth cause that your bosom burn (more intense vibrating) within you is an amazing confirming and revealing experience.

RESONATION

Where quickening is the stronger jolt to confirm a truth or redirect your life to be in harmony with your foreordination, resonation is a softer, guiding feeling. Resonation is the experience of vibrating in harmony with light, truth, and intelligences and being aware of the companionship of the Holy Ghost. It is knowing that you are following a path of progression.

The language of the universe from the perspective of theoretical physics is really in a form of vibrations or frequencies.[5] If you want to know a gospel truth or if you need to know which direction to turn, then you will vibrate at the same frequency as the truth or the direction. Perhaps the best way to understand how resonation works comes from a personal account of my elementary school years.

> My first-grade teacher was Miss Slack. One day, she stood in front of the class and talked about sound. She struck a tuning fork and asked if we could hear it. We could. She then explained how the sound waves were making our eardrums vibrate, which transmitted messages to our brains. To make the point that sound was something real, she again struck the tuning fork. She then brought up a second tuning fork that was not vibrating. She placed the new tuning fork about six inches from the vibrating fork. The second tuning fork started to vibrate just by being next to the vibrating tuning fork. She stopped the vibrations from the first turning fork, and the second one kept the sound alive.

Resilient saints are those who make choices based upon the options to which you resonate. You will feel the rightness of your choice with soft, gentle vibrations in your soul much like the second tuning fork. Another detail of Miss Slack's tuning fork experiment was that the second tuning fork was the same size as the first. If the tuning fork had been bigger or smaller, the second tuning fork would not have vibrated with the same intensity. The metaphor for us suggests that we are walking in a world of glory with all the answers to life challenges, and we must be in a state of humility and readiness to receive the truth in its fullness. If we are "bigger" that the sweet vibrations coming from the Spirit, the vibrations of the Spirit will have little impact. By bigger I mean that we rely upon our "expert" mind and conscious logic and think we know more than the gentle Spirit of truth.

Every truth and every best answer will be disclosed through the universal and subtle vibrational language of resonation. You resonate to music that makes you feel good. You resonate to nature that makes you feel peaceful. You resonate to projects that you enjoy. Resonation is the soft and gentle assurance that you are progressing to fulfill your foreordination and following a path of glory.

Sometimes we resonate to our progressive path of glory, and the softer vibrations may not even be part of our awareness. You can feel, though, the peace and sense that you are on the right path, making the right decisions, and in harmony with your foreordination, yet you may not be sure exactly where you are going. That's OK to be in the flow of life's soft progressive pathway. Nephi, who was trying to follow the path of his foreordination followed the spirit blindly.

> And I was led by the Spirit, not knowing beforehand the things which I should do. (1 Nephi 4:6)

Even in other cultures we see validation that we are being gently guided by a spirit field of energy. In Eastern philosophies, the energy field that guides us is God's Spirit, but they call it qi as the right path is called the Tao. Lao Tzu, in the *Tao Te Ching*, states:

> One who lives in accordance with nature does not go against the way of things. He moves in harmony with the present moment, always knowing the truth of just what to do.[6]

Try to remember what it feels like to resonate as you walk your subtle path with glory. Remember the feelings of rightness or peace when you are feeling, thinking, and doing in harmony with your foreordination. Remember a time, or even perhaps now, when you felt the subtle peace and guidance of the Spirit.

1. Can you feel the peace and rightness of your career? Does it seem that you were made to do what you are doing? Are you resonating to that choice?
2. Can you feel the peace and rightness of the gospel principles? Are you resonating to that choice?
3. Can you feel the peace and rightness of choosing your friends or spouse?
4. Can you feel the Spirit in your home? Are there rooms to which you resonate more than others?
5. Do you resonate to your life? Does it have purpose and meaning?

The following are examples of spiritual promptings in the form of the soft vibrations and resonation. It is difficult to describe the experience of resonation because it is personal and the intensity varies from person to person. The sections that follow highlight the multiple ways that the Lord can lead us by the hand as we resonate to the Spirit.

Still Small Voice

Boyd K. Packer defined the experience of personal revelation:

> The Holy Ghost speaks with a voice that you *feel* more than you *hear*. It is described as a "still small voice." And while we speak of "listening" to the whisperings of the Spirit, most often one describes a spiritual prompting by saying, "I had a *feeling*. . . ." . . .
>
> Revelation comes as words we *feel* more than *hear*. Nephi told his wayward brothers, who were visited by an angel, "Ye were past *feeling*, that ye could not *feel* his words." The scriptures are full of such expressions as "The veil was taken from our minds, and the eyes of our understanding were opened," or "I will tell you in your mind and in your heart," or "I did enlighten thy mind," or "Speak the thoughts that I shall put into your hearts." There are hundreds of verses which teach of revelation.[7]

EPIPHANIES AND GESTALTS

Epiphanies and gestalts are "ah ha" moments or what we sometimes call the eureka effect. Sometimes you feel energized when new ideas jump into your mind. An epiphany is a sudden new perception or insight into the meaning of something. It is a burst of understanding. The epiphany is more than just an idea, and it is accompanied with a stirring of your whole soul (quickening), confirming the importance of the idea. It is a sudden burst of understanding when previously your thoughts lacked focus.

As you are pondering your disruption in life as part of the resilient journey, an epiphany may jump into your head, and if it is accompanied with the resonating confirmation, it is something that you should consider. The classic example in history is the story of Sir Isaac Newton, the famous mathematician and physicist, who observed an apple falling from a tree. He noticed how the apple seemed to accelerate as it fell. The epiphany of the falling apple in 1687 led to Newton's discovery of the universal law of gravity.

A gestalt is the ability of your mind and spirit to create a big picture inclusive of the many individual pieces when all the pieces of a complex problem come together. It is a time when God again in Doctrine and Covenants 112:10 can "lead thee by the hand, and give thee answers to thy prayers" in these gestalt moments.

In psychology, a gestalt is also known as a law of simplicity. Gestalt theorists followed the basic principle that the whole is greater than the sum of its parts. In other words, with the vision of your purpose in life, which is to harvest glory to become worthy of the first resurrection, individual life problems and challenges are viewed as minor in the big picture. In the language of the gestalt therapist in viewing the "whole," a cognitive process takes place and the mind makes a leap from comprehending the parts to realizing the whole. We visually and psychologically attempt to make order out of chaos, to create harmony or structure from seemingly disconnected bits of information.

It is the climax of the life disruption or chaos when suddenly all the parts of the puzzle make sense. It is the magical moment of clarity. On a larger scale, it is a quickening moment when you have a vision of your life. From chapter 10 of *Teachings of the Presidents of the Church: Joseph Smith*, we read the following:

> A person may profit by noticing the first intimation of the spirit of revelation; for instance, when you feel pure intelligence flowing into you, it may give you sudden strokes of ideas, so that by noticing it, you may find it fulfilled the same day or soon; . . . those things that were presented unto your minds by the Spirit of God, will come to pass; and thus by learning the Spirit of God and understanding it, you may grow into the principle of revelation, until you become perfect in Christ Jesus.[8]

RECURRING THOUGHTS

Sometimes the Spirit prompts you to action by sending messages to your conscious mind (intellectual resilience) over and over again until they are heard. The experience of having recurring thoughts is often a message of great importance coming from the greater wisdom of the Holy Ghost. When recurring thoughts occur, it is a good time to stop and ponder to discover the meaning in the recurring thoughts. You can anticipate an infusion of glory with an epiphany.

SPIRITUAL PROMPTS AND HUNCHES

A spiritual prompting is a soft quickening moment that is sometimes referred to as inspiration, intuition, or gut feeling. Spiritual prompts are moments that provide you with answers to life challenges and problems. The prompts come with sudden resonating vibrations and energy. It feels very right and very good. When choosing a direction in life, if you study something for a while and it is accompanied by a strong resonating feeling of joy and rightness, it is a good path. Intuition or gut feelings are terms that also describe spiritual prompts as the ability to sense or know something without a rational reason. For example, the feeling you get when you first meet someone may be an instant sense of trust with accompanied joy. Conversely, you may get an instant feeling of distrust, caution, or fear. A softer term for the spiritual prompt is a hunch.

SYNCHRONICITY OR COINCIDENCES

Synchronicity is a term coined by the great psychologist Carl Jung. Synchronicity is when you put meaning to coincidences that occur in your life. For example, perhaps you have been thinking about a friend you have not talked to for some time, and you unexpectedly run into him or her at a store. Perhaps you have been pondering a challenge in your life and you happen to be watching a movie that is a metaphor for your own life situation. You leave the movie with an approach to deal with the challenge. When you are open to synchronistic events, they can help you make choices in your life because they are a form of guidance from a greater wisdom than your conscious mind. Synchronicity is a quickening moment.

FLOW

In academic literature, we read of this subtle guidance using such descriptors as *flow* or the *path with heart*. Mihaly Csíkszentmihályi speaks of *flow* as a state of concentration or complete absorption with the activity at hand and with the situation.[9] It is a state in which you are so involved in an activity that nothing else seems to matter. When you are striving to understand the scriptures, time flies. Every action, movement, and thought follows a previous insight and you are guided along a path that harvests glory. Flow is the gentle accumulation of light and truth a little at a time as you become engrossed in glory-laden activities or thoughts.

RECORD YOUR RESONATING AND QUICKENING MOMENTS

When you have quickening moments or when you resonate to a truth, be sure to write them down as soon as possible. So many answers to prayers come at odd times—not necessarily when you are on your knees. Sometimes you wake in the night with spiritual prompts that resonate to your life situation. Some of them quicken your soul.

It is important to write the prompts down because so many times when you wake up in the morning, the impactful spirit is gone and you have forgotten the full impact of the glory-filled messages. Sometimes you are driving or walking somewhere—again, it is wise to write these personal revelations down to help you.

Discernment

But how do we discern whether the "burning in our bosoms" is through the Holy Ghost or the result of more carnal emotions, anger, or passions? There are several checkpoints to verify that personal revelation comes from God.

During your preparation to receive personal revelations as well as the aftermath of feeling energy and motivation of resonating and quickening moments, it is important to discern whether the insight you have received is genuine or not. Discernment is a difficult challenge if mixed emotions are involved. How do we discern between a choice of our own gratification with accompanying short-term physical pleasure or quick fix as compared to a resonating and quickening moment that will allow for an infusion of glory? Consider the following resonating confirmations to assure your answers come from the matrix of God's glory. Let me suggest six checkpoints: progression, outcome, peace, infringement, character, and staying power.

1. **Progression:** Remember that progression is the accumulation of glory, light, and truth throughout your lifetime. Ask yourself the question, "Am I harvesting glory if I adopt and implement this plan of action?"

2. **Outcome:** Consider the immediate outcome of your inspiration. Does it feel peaceful and make sense for you? If you still have a stupor of thought, then perhaps you should either wait or explore other options.

3. **Peace:** As you ponder the action or thought, is there a resonating feeling of peace? If it does not have peace, then it may not be a path of glory.

4. **Infringement:** Would your actions or thoughts unjustly infringe upon the rights or peace of others? If they do, then you may need to consider other options.

5. **Character:** As you consider your character resilience, ask yourself these questions about the insight you have received: "Does it fit within my character code of thought and action? Does the insight embrace integrity, honesty, honor, fairness, loyalty, fidelity, and kindness and lie within my moral framework?" If not, it may not be a genuine revelation. It is difficult to imagine the conflict of morals and quickening prompts that Nephi experienced when faced with the decision to kill Laban.

6. **Staying power:** A solution from the Spirit will continue over time. Reflection upon the personal resonation or quickening moment will continue to feel good. As you ponder the insight, you will continue to feel peace.

THE TIMING OF PERSONAL REVELATION

Sometimes becoming a resilient saint requires patience—sometimes a little patience or sometimes a lot of patience. You may have done all that you can do and not receive an answer, but then the next day when you are working through your daily activities, you have a quickening moment. With a lot of patience, we may need to consider the natural order of things.

Among the many powerful quotes that came from Elder Neal A. Maxwell, this classic quote perfectly describes this principle:

> Faith also includes trust in God's timing, for He has said, "All things must come to pass in their time" (D&C 64:32). Ironically, some who acknowledge God are tried by His timing, globally and personally![10]

You continue to harvest glory throughout your life. For some of the bigger rewards, you have to wait for nature's timing. A young person may dream of serving people by becoming a physician, but at this point only has a high school education. Answers come with patience and in some cases hard work or maturity. Let's review the metaphor of planting the seed.

> In order to harvest the fruit from a garden, you have to trust in the timing of nature. You need to assure that it is the growing season and the environment is right (ecological resilience). You need to prepare the soil and assure it is nurturing and then plant the seed and cover it with some dirt to protect it from the sun and other elements. You need to provide water to stimulate growth and over time let it be the life source for the plant. You need to protect it from the weeds or bad habits. Over time, the plant will break through the surface of the soil, and you continue to nurture until the plant becomes full grown. Then, after weeks of nurturing, the buds of fruit begin to appear. Again, patience is necessary to assure ripening. Picking too early will result in a bitter fruit. When nature tells you it is time, the fruit will be ripe and ready to enjoy. The same is true with the timing harvesting glory.

I love some of the quotes from great thinkers in the world.

- Do you have the patience to wait till your mud settles and the water is clear? Can you remain unmoving till the right action arises by itself?

  —Lao Tzu[11]

- Adopt the pace of Nature. Her secret is patience.

  —Ralph Waldo Emerson[12]

- To lose patience is to lose the battle.

  —Mahatma Gandhi[13]

- Patience is power; with time and patience, the mulberry leaf becomes silk.

  —Chinese proverb[14]

- *La Patience est amere, mais son fruit est doux.* (Patience is bitter, but its fruit is sweet.)

  —Jean Chardin[15]

On the other hand, sometimes quickening moments come with urgency. In crisis situations, you may not have time for readiness, and answers may come very quickly.

> When my little brother, Victor, was about four or five years old, an experience happened that confirmed the power of resonation—mother's intuition. One day, as Mom was hanging out the clothes on a clothesline, an intuitive prompt—or, more accurately, a bolt of warning—consumed her whole being. She suddenly felt fear for Victor, and her heart started to race. On the little five-acre homestead, she could have gone anywhere. She could have gone into the house, to the horses, to the cows, or to the neighbors', but her quickening moment prompted her to run the one hundred yards to the south part of the property to the nutria cesspool. (We raised nutria animals for their pelts.) When she got there, little Victor had just fallen and was struggling to get out. He was slipping and kept falling back into the smelly, watery nutria waste. Victor was in trouble, repeatedly sinking below the surface. Mom arrived just in time to pull him out by the hair of his head. As she dragged him to safety, she hosed him down and put him in a bathtub for a thorough cleaning. When Victor was finally safe in his room, Mom went to her room and burst into tears. She was so grateful she had listened to her mother's intuition and acted in the nick of time.

Sometimes No Answer Is the Answer

If you are seeking confirming light and truth to accompany a decision or to take an action and you continue to be confused, you may have received an answer from God. If none of your choices are accompanied with resonation or quickening, then your answer may be either to do nothing, to do something else, or to be patient for the right time. A stupor of thought generally indicates none of your options is the right option or the right time for the option. While translating the Book of Mormon, Joseph received this revelation in Doctrine and Covenants 9:9 that teaches us that we should not proceed with a stupor of thought:

> But if it be not right you shall have no such feelings, but you shall have a stupor of thought that shall cause you to forget the thing which is wrong; therefore, you cannot write that which is sacred save it be given you from me.

If you are confused about a relationship and you have a stupor of thought about making a commitment, the time may not be right. If you are preparing a talk and experience a stupor of thought, you may need to consider a different method. You may need a different story or a different scriptural approach. If you are wondering what to say to someone during a clear disagreement and you have a stupor of thought, it is better to wait until you connect to a resonating approach to the conversation.

GIFTS OF THE SPIRIT

For resonating and quickening moments to guide you, you should also explore your gifts of the Spirit. We read in Doctrine and Covenants 46:17–25 about some of the gifts that will help you harvest glory to become more unbreakable.

> And again, verily I say unto you, to some is given, by the Spirit of God, the word of wisdom.
>
> To another is given the word of knowledge, that all may be taught to be wise and to have knowledge.
>
> And again, to some it is given to have faith to be healed;
>
> And to others it is given to have faith to heal.
>
> And again, to some is given the working of miracles;
>
> And to others it is given to prophesy;
>
> And to others the discerning of spirits.

> And again, it is given to some to speak with tongues;
> And to another is given the interpretation of tongues.

As you ponder some of the gifts of the Spirit, think about which gifts and others you might have. You may read more about your gifts in your patriarchal blessings and how these gifts can help you with resonating and quickening. If you have the gift of the word of wisdom, what does that really mean in helping your make wise choices? How can the gift of knowledge, the faith to be healed, and the working of miracles help you to receive answers to prayer? Using your unique gifts to make wise choices for your whole soul will help you to become a resilient saint. Hopefully, you will learn to recognize the many gifts and the other resonating and quickening forms of personal revelation so that you can be led by the hand.

THE APPLIED THEOLOGY OF EVERYTHING

You are living in an amazing mortal experience with the opportunity of harvesting glory to the point where you will be worthy of the terrestrial kingdom initially and then ultimately the celestial kingdom. During this mortality, the Lord has blessed you with plentiful sources and a range of experiences to recognize and celebrate the infusions of glory. The glory in every important thing is to become more aware of gestalts, of synchronicities, of peace when doing daily activities, and of the glory in your gifts of the Spirit. All of the experiences of glory can become a Simba moment.

NOTES

1. *The Lion King*, directed by Roger Allers and Rob Minkoff (Burbank, CA: Buena Vista Pictures, 1994.), DVD.
2. Dallin H. Oaks, "Revelation" (Brigham Young University devotional, September 29, 1981), speeches.byu.edu.
3. Mihaly Csíkszentmihályi, *Finding Flow: The Psychology of Engagement with Everyday Life* (New York: Basic Books, 1997).
4. Carl Jung, "The Concept of the Collective Unconscious," in *The Collected Works of C. G. Jung*, vol. 9, *The Archetypes and the Collective Unconscious* (Princeton: Princeton University Press, 1968), 44.
5. Brian Greene, *The Elegant Universe*, directed by Joseph McMaster, David Hickman, and Julia Cort, aired September 28, 2003 (Boston: NOVA, 2003), http://www.pbs.org/wgbh/nova/physics/elegant-universe.html.
6. Lao Tzu, *Tao Te Ching: The New Translation*, trans. Jonathan Star (New York: Penguin, 2008), 9.
7. Boyd K. Packer, "Personal Revelation: The Gift, the Test, and the Promise," *Ensign*, November 1994, 59.
8. Joseph Smith, *Teachings of the Presidents of the Church: Joseph Smith* (2011), 129.
9. Mihaly Csíkszentmihályi, *Finding Flow: The Psychology of Engagement with Everyday Life* (New York: Basic Books, 1997).
10. Neal A. Maxwell, "Lest Ye Be Wearied and Faint in Your Minds," *Ensign*, May 1991, 88.
11. Lao Tzu in Joseph A. Magno, *The Spiritual Philosophy of the Tao Te Ching* (Chicago: Pendragon Publishing, 2005), 90.
12. Ralph Waldo Emerson, *Lectures and Biographical Sketches* (Cambridge: The Riverside Press, 1886), 152.
13. Mahatma Gandhi, *Teachings of Mahatma Gandhi* (Lahore: Indian Printing Works, 1947), 439.
14. "A Thought for Every Day," *Milady Beautiful* 8, no. 4 (January 1919), 42.
15. Jean Chardin, *Voyages en Perse et autres lieux de l'Orient* [Journeys in Persia and other places of the East] (Amsterdam: chez Jean Louis de Lorme, 1711), 175.

8

Self-Mastery and the Art of Becoming an Unbreakable Saint

Identity formation is the experience of creating and assuming optimal natures to help conquer unique life challenges to add to one's existing treasury of identities created through previously resiliently reintegrating after disruptions.

An example in nature of the resilient journey and the adoption of identities is to witness the fascinating journey in the life cycle of the salmon. The salmon demonstrates amazing grit and persistence after being prompted by Mother Nature. From the salmon life cycle, we will see many parallels in our lives.

> Adult females spawn and deposit eggs in the sands of creeks in the tops of the mountains. The eggs hatch, and in a few weeks, the little salmon, called *alevin*, initially feed from the yokes of the eggs from which they are hatched. When the nourishment from the egg

runs out, the tiny fish change their identity again and become a *fry*. Fry learn to feed on the carcasses of adult salmon who have already spawned and died.

Over time, a new identity emerges—that of a *smolt*. The smolt experiences a physiological change to prevent salt water from entering its blood. The smolt has the amazing capacity to live in both fresh and salt water. With that potential, the smolt journeys downstream. The creeks grow into small streams, and the streams grow into rivers. The smolt become salmon, and after drifting for hundreds of miles, they enter their ocean life.

It is fascinating how salmon can live in both fresh water and salt water. The salmon stay in the ocean for a couple of years doing whatever teenaged salmon do and maturing into adult salmon. When the adult fish have finished maturing in the ocean, then something magical strikes their intrinsic wiring. They have a powerful quickening urge to return to where they were hatched in the mountains. They seek out the mouth of the rivers from which they emerged years earlier and begin the journey back home.

It is interesting to witness that at this time in the experience of the salmon that they continue to have identity changes. The change from a bright silver color to a deep, bold red as mature adults. The drive of Mother Nature, analogous to the human spirit, is so powerful that they will fight against great odds to complete the life cycle. At first, the rivers are gentle with currents of only three or four miles an hour, but as the elevation rises toward the mountain, the water comes faster and faster, and the salmon have to fight to make progress. Perhaps the biggest challenge comes from the waterfalls that salmon have to jump. This is where we see the famous salmon runs and watch these

> fish jump, fight, and climb the falls because of the power of their drive—their self-mastery—their spirit.
>
> Finally, the survivors are beaten, exhausted, and near dead, and they finish their journey by finding the place of their birth in the small creeks. Their remaining energy is put solely into the production of eggs for females and milt (sperm) for males. The mature adults, with all the energy they can muster, lay and fertilize their eggs and die shortly thereafter. Their carcasses fertilize the algae and become the food for the little salmon (fry) to eat, and the cycle starts all over again.

Granted, salmon are simple and act mostly on instinct, but still the quickening moments that help them evolve and form a series of new identities throughout their life cycle parallel your life. To magically leave their adult and mature life in the ocean and turn back to spawn and die at their place of origin high in the mountains is an amazing example of quickening. The powerful quickening moment compelled them to swim upstream with a mission and purpose. I recognize that I am reading too much into the instinctual nature of a salmon, but the choice to head back upstream rather than live in the comfort zone of the ocean is amazing. If they had the capacity to choose, how many salmon would choose to stay and play in the vastness of the oceans? We, too, have the agency to fulfill our greater mission in life based upon our quickening with glory experiences. We, too, can develop new identities to becoming dogged and relentless resilient saints to swim upstream to fulfill our foreordination.

At this point along your mortal resilient journey, you can now emerge from the trough of your disruption and emerge with glory, inspiration and hope. With that bit of glory, you know the path you should take and now with persistence, grit, and dogged tenacity follow that path to its conclusion. On the resiliency model below, you can see where self-mastery (box 6) lies along the resilient journey.

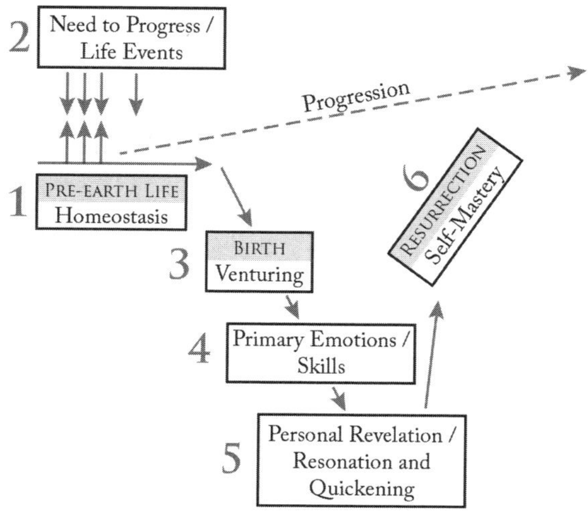

Elder James E. Faust said, "Self-mastery cannot be bought by money or fame. It is the ultimate test of our character. It requires climbing out of the deep valleys of our lives and scaling our own Mount Everests."[1] It is also the ultimate test of our resilient spirit and our ability to conquer life challenges. Self-mastery is the quality that makes the difference between being breakable or unbreakable. The chapter will describe self-mastery as (1) quickening and creating the image of new identity, (2) agency to become the identity, (3) the art of becoming the new identity, (4) mustering the grit to persist with the identity, and (5) maintaining the luster of your treasury of identities.

Quickening and the Image of an Identity

Whether the disruptions in your life are minor or major, each experience allows you the opportunity to increase your self-mastery and become stronger and more resilient.

Quickening gives a magical glimpse of your new identity that will thrive in the wake of your current disruptive challenge. The embodiment of that identity is conceived in persistence and grit.

With the quickening infusion of light, truth, and intelligences, you have a picture in your mind of how the next phase of your resilient journey should look. Like an evolving salmon, an image of a new identity will be formed in your mind. Quickening creates an image of what you need to be or what you need to do. You may catch a glimpse of an image that you need to acquire as you witness someone else who is successfully coping and thriving with your life challenge. For example, in a particular situation, you may need to be more assertive, but the same identity may not be required in another situation when you might access another identity, such as being more compassionate.

You have the potential to formulate any helpful identity that comes to you through the light and intelligences that come from a quickening experience. To repeat, and to make sure that you are clear, the identity you are going to create is one of many identities that are within the treasury of your life experiences and become part of your personality. It will be an identity to deal with a selected challenge.

There are no negative identities that you can adopt if you have experienced a confirming resonation from intelligences and glory that it is right for a specific situation. The "if" in the previous sentence is big. There are many hurtful identities, such as being unreliable or a deceiver, but these are not likely accompanied with glory. Some identities may appear questionable, but in the right situation, they are accompanied with the Spirit. Nephi was not a murderer, but to see him kill a drunken Laban, an observer would condemn him. But Nephi was quickened to violate the most basic commandment in order to fulfill the quickening of the Spirit. Captain Moroni killed many Lamanites for the sake of the preservation of the people. Abraham as a father would have never assumed the identity of a murderer but still was ready to kill his son Isaac. Obviously, the Spirit has to be amazingly overwhelming to violate the basic commandments.

Some identities are behaviorally related, such as changing your identity from being inactive in the Church to becoming active, a smoker to a nonsmoker, or a nonexerciser to an exerciser. Other identities refer to qualities as you resonate to being a more patient person in a particular situation or being more energetic in another. In our own lives, quickening may bring different identities to deal with the particular situation. For example, the "rebel" identity may be considered negative, but in the situation where you have to get away from negative influences and temptations, then the rebel identity is the identity the Lord would have you become in that situation. Consider a disruptive challenge you may be facing and consider which of the following identities may be part of your quickening moment.

- Do you need to be more of a believer or a skeptic?
- Do you need to be more of an optimist or pessimist?
- Do you need to be more patient or demanding?
- Do you need to be more humble or confident?
- Do you need to be more powerful or vulnerable?
- Do you need to be more of a conservative or liberal?
- Do you need to be more of a planner or spontaneous?
- Do you need to be more flexible or steadfast?
- Do you need to be more of a warrior or a peacemaker?
- Do you need to be more of a giver or a receiver?
- Do you need to be more fun-loving or more serious?
- Do you need to be more of a leader or a follower?
- Do you need to be more loyal or rebellious?
- Do you need to be more of an introvert or an extrovert?
- Do you need to be more of a creator or a destroyer?

In the right situation, you can be all of these. You may need to destroy pornographic images. You may make a sustaining vote to be a loyal follower of a newly chosen leader that you do not necessarily like. In a crisis situation, you may need to be more demanding that normal.

> I remember a time when my son was having difficulty trying to study for an exam when he was in the eighth grade. He was going to have a test the next day about the cultures of the world in a geography class. So I decided to do my parenting role and sat down to encourage him to study.
>
> As I asked him about what he was studying, I realized that it had been a long time since I had learned anything about the cultures in Africa. So, as a parent who made a living teaching university classes, I went to my treasury of identities and brought up my student identity, which is one that I use often but generally not in the role of a parent. I said, "Brannon, I don't think I know very much about the cultures in Africa, can you teach me?" Brannon's countenance brightened as he took on the identity of teacher and began to instruct me on what he knew and then looked up answers for those he didn't know.

You have already created numerous identities in your lifetime, and you have an armory of identities housed within you. Each time you have faced a challenge and have overcome it, you have a new identity. Each new identity is like an additional piece of iron that you put on your full suit of armor. You worked through a hard project and created the identity of a hard worker. Hard worker is a piece of metal to add to your coat of armor. As an adolescent, the first time you resisted peers that were trying to get you to drink, you created the identity of a principled young person—another piece of iron for your suit of armor. At work, when the opportunity came to steal some office supplies and you refrained, you created an identity of being an honest person.

Each new experience creates a new identity that could be riveted upon your coat of armor. You become more unbreakable with the more conquering experiences that you have and consequently are able to place more protective metal on your armor of God.

> Wherefore take unto you the whole armour of God, that ye may be able to withstand in the evil day, and having done all, to stand.
> Stand therefore, having your loins girt about with truth, and having on the breastplate of righteousness;
> And your feet shod with the preparation of the gospel of peace;
> Above all, taking the shield of faith, wherewith ye shall be able to quench all the fiery darts of the wicked.
> And take the helmet of salvation, and the sword of the Spirit, which is the word of God:
> Praying always with all prayer and supplication in the Spirit, and watching thereunto with all perseverance and supplication for all saints. (Ephesians 6:13–18)

Agency to Become the Identity

Many people catch glimpses of new identities that will help them progress and harvest glory in their lives. They receive an insight as to how to become stronger through their adversities, and yet in the wake of life's routine or perhaps through lack of courage, the quickening moment fades. You have the agency to choose to create that identity.

Agency is a mortal human freedom that allows you to choose what to think, how to feel, and what you want to do in life's situations. You can use the freedom to harvest glory in the second estate or you have the agency to watch your glory begin to lose its splendor.

If you have resonated to an identity, then it is important for you to choose to become that new identity. You have a choice to act or not to act. Robert D. Hales stated the following:

> Agency allows us to be tested and tried to see whether or not we will endure to the end and return to our Heavenly Father with honor. . . . Agency permits us to make faithful, obedient choices that strengthen us so that we can lift and strengthen others.[2]

Agency to seek and harvest glory in our thoughts and actions is a function of a balancing scales. With every decision, you weigh the two sides of the scale.

On the side that will help you harvest glory that is in harmony with your foreordination and mission on earth, you will see your resilient forces. You will see the energy and power of your childlike character and noble yearnings and drives. You will feel the power of your nurturing environment and you will strengthen your spiritual connection to the Father through your universal resilient drives. You will also feel the yearning to nurture your mortal body to function as optimally as you can with exercise, sleep, and nutrition. You are stocked with spiritual and essential drives that will guide you to be wise with your agency.

On the other side of the scale are your mortal temptations and passions. The scale is loaded with a variety of worldly quick-fix pleasures that compromise your foreordination. These are the quick-fix pleasures of the world that result in glory-draining, guilt, and sadness.

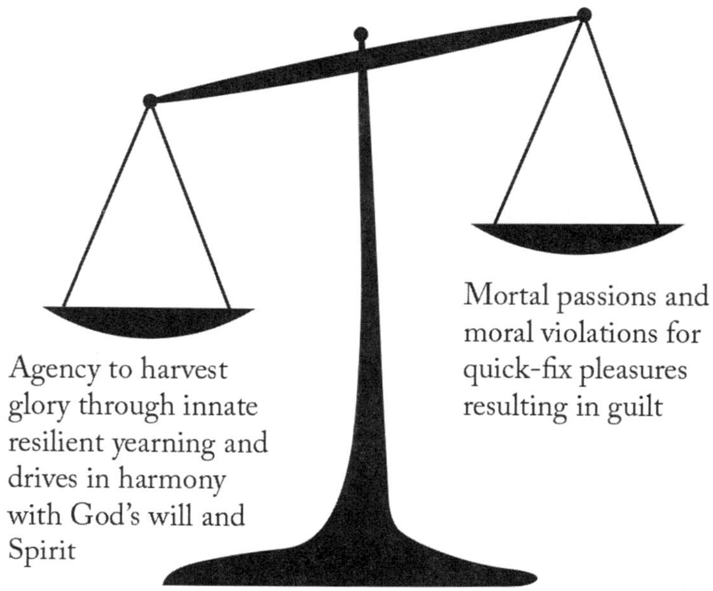

We discussed earlier how the mind is the control center. You have the power to choose glory or darkness. Even in the direst circumstances, you can choose to embrace or reject the love and light of the Savior. Sometimes we blame others for our choices, but the reality is that really cannot deflect the blame. The agency is ours.

I hope we do not forget the great messages and inspiration that came from Viktor Frankl after the wisdom he harvested from his experiences in a Nazi concentration camp during World War II. Dr. Frankl was an Austrian neurologist and psychiatrist as well as a Holocaust survivor. In the trough of despair and suffering beyond anything most of us can image, Dr. Frankl had a major quickening experience and received great insights into the agency of mortality. Dr. Frankl's book *Man's Search for Meaning* chronicled his experience and horrific suffering in the concentration camp. He cites how he watched those that had purpose and meaning survive and those that did not have purpose fail and die. He realized that agency is the ultimate human freedom. He defined it as choosing an attitude in any given situation.

> Everything can be taken from a man but one thing: the last of the human freedoms—to choose one's attitude in any given set of circumstances, to choose one's own way. And there were always choices to make. Every day, every hour, offered the opportunity to make a decision, a decision which determined whether you would or would not submit to those powers which threatened to rob you of your very self, your inner freedom.[3]

If you get insight into what you should do in your life situation, the choice to do it is based upon the value you put on it.

The Art of Becoming the New Identity

It is clear that there are a variety of disruptions in every person's life. I will try to describe this imagery strategy in very general terms with the hope that you can fill in the detail. The imagery guidance that will be given will help you to overcome a bad habit or adopt a more positive quality. Your identity may be to become a more unbreakable saint. This strategy will help you to create a new identity that will help with resisting temptation to become unbreakable.

I am going to assume that your belief to become the new identity may be a little weak at this point, so we will go through three progressive imagery strategies, beginning with the easiest. It is best to read the imagery strategy and then close your eyes and live the suggested scenarios. In a comfortable position, when there are no distractions, try the following:

Imagery 1: Hero Observance

I want you to imagine that you are in a movie theater all by yourself. As you watch the screen, you will see a movie of the challenge you have in your life, and to deal with it, you need to acquire a new identity.

You see the life challenge on the screen. Take a moment and imagine a hero or heroine that is going to take on the same challenge that you are facing. The hero can be anyone who would handle situations like the way you wish you could. You can bring in the Savior as your hero. You can bring in prophets and heroes from the stories in the scriptures. You can reflect on your ancestors you have learned about in your genealogy and let them be the hero. You can imagine presidencies of the Relief Society or the general authorities.

You will watch as clearly as your imagination will allow to witness the hero demonstrate the key quality that you need to conquer your life challenge. Be sure that the figure is someone who exemplifies a resilient saint who is conquering life challenges. You watch your imaginary movie screen as your hero is blazing a trail and modeling for you the identity you need to acquire to optimally conquer the challenge. You are watching to know how in your real life the identity will help you to become what you want to become. Watch, using as many senses as you can, the hero acting, behaving, and doing what you wish to do. Watch this person over and over again in your mind, demonstrating the quality you want to acquire in your new identity.

Take a moment to reflect upon what you saw. What were the key qualities from the modeling that you saw? Write that here.

IMAGERY 2: THIRD-PARTY OBSERVER

> Now you will change the scene. Imagine now that you are still in the movie but you are that hero in the movie you just watched. Watch yourself become the identity. Watch how you connect with glory. See your courage, your humility, your social skills, and your persistence, or think and become whatever quality you want or need. Watch yourself doing what the hero did, whether it is struggling to overcome a bad habit or becoming more attuned to the Spirit.
>
> Rehearse this scene over and over in your mind, making the image of you with the new identity as clear as possible, including sounds, colors, and movement in your imagery. Continue to watch again and again in your imagination as you demonstrate that identity.

Again, write your thoughts here as you watched yourself as an observer. How did it make you feel?

Imagery 3: The Art of Becoming

Again, in the same situation, after watching your hero and witnessing your own self becoming the new identity, now you will become that identity.

> Imagine now that you are in your life situation that you have just witnessed; however, you now see the situation out of your own eyes. You can feel the power and glory of the identity you are becoming. You can feel your innate resilience—particularly the glory from your first estate. You can feel your resilient spirit becoming infused with the spirit of the new identity.
>
> As you sense the nature of the identity, you become it, and your body feels the strength to do what you need to do. Your human spirit is reminding you of the quickening moment, energizing you to do what you need to do. Your mind has a vision of what you need to do. Walk through the situation and become the identity you need to become. Rehearse the scene over and over in your mind.

Write your thoughts and feelings about your experience.

The last step is obviously to go out and be the identity in real life. Feel it and act upon it. It will require grit and persistence over time to have the identity become a part of your arsenal of identities. With the glory of the soul and the glory from all around you, you can become the new identity.

Mustering Grit to Persist in the Identity

Like the pioneers leaving Nauvoo, we too need to take leaps of faith. Your planning and imagining is preparation for becoming unbreakable. If your spirit and your mind are in sync, then you can become the identity that you need to become to conquer your life challenges. President Spencer W. Kimball used to say, "Just do it." The glory, the light, the truth, and your resilient drives are amazingly powerful if you will let them lead the charge to become the identity you need to become.

Resilient reintegration now becomes finding your grit and persistence in adopting the identity that you need to become an unbreakable saint. Much has been said about the importance of persistence and grit. Grit is the stick-to-itiveness or work required to adopt a new identity. It is so easy to quit or give up. Persistence over time becomes a habit and therefore an identity of finding grit in all your challenges. Persistent grit facilitates the experience of becoming what you want to become. Grit is the perseverance of effort to accomplish a long-term goal, or in this case, assume a new identity, no matter what obstacles or challenges lay in your path. The following scriptures promise great blessing of endurance and self-mastery:

> And then, if thou endure it well, God shall exalt thee on high; thou shalt triumph over all thy foes. (D&C 121:8)

> Beareth all things, believeth all things, hopeth all things, endureth all things. (1 Corinthians 13:7)

> And blessed are they who shall seek to bring forth my Zion at that day, for they shall have the gift and the power of the Holy Ghost; and if they endure unto the end they shall be lifted up at the last day, and shall be saved in the everlasting kingdom of the Lamb; and whoso shall publish peace, yea, tidings of great joy, how beautiful upon the mountains shall they be. (1 Nephi 13:37)

President Heber J. Grant was known for often repeating this quote attributed to Ralph Waldo Emerson:

> That which we persist in doing becomes easier for us to do—not that the nature of the thing is changed, but that our power to do is increased.[4]

The more that you exercise the identity in your selected situation, it does become easier. As you ponder the identity that has emerged from your quickening experience, you can think about how your resilient drives help you to have the grit and persistence to become that identity.

Most parents try to teach their children to grow up with positive identities. They teach great lessons and help you form identities. They want you to create the identity of a hard workers to thrive in this world. My parents were great role models of hard work and lovingly expected us to become hard workers. We lived on a couple of acres of land which brought numerous chores and responsibilities. One of my lessons as a child came from working on our little ranch.

> Living on a small homestead allowed us to raise some animals and raise vegetables and fruits in a garden. The curse of curses to our huge garden was what we called devil grass (Bermuda grass). This nasty weed would grow all over the ground and put down long and strong roots even in the heat of summer without water. When you pulled the grass out, it would break and the roots would grow more grass in several

> days. I hated devil grass. After the garden was growing pretty well, devil grass would always creep in, and Dad's gentle nudging on a Saturday morning would be, "Buzz, could you get that devil grass out of the garden today?" Make me mow the lawn, shovel manure, take out the trash, dig ditches, but please don't make me pull the devil grass!
>
> I would start weeding on a row in the dry dirt and, predictably, the tops of the grass would break off and I would have to dig down and get those roots out. I would celebrate each inch that I was able to clear. It seemed like forever for me to be done with one row and then there was another row to do. Amazingly, using most of the day, the garden would be free of devil grass by evening.
>
> I have reflected again and again about my battle with devil grass. I would sometimes wonder why I didn't give up. The prevalent theme was because I loved and valued my father's opinion so much that I would even endure devil grass to make my dad proud. This is the great lesson that my gentle father taught me as a child—that you can accomplish almost anything with grit and persistence. That lesson has carried me through athletics, academics, and my profession. (But I still hate devil grass.)

The identity that my father wanted me to have was that of a hard worker. He gave me an experience in which I would have to access all my spiritual resilient drives to accomplish what I had to accomplish. As a young teenager, I have reflected upon how naturally I used my resilient drives to have energy to weed the devil grass.

- **Childlike resilience:** I used to make a game of seeing how fast I could weed a foot of dirt of the garden. I'd start and begin counting until the foot was clear of devil grass. It became a game of sorts trying to beat my time.

- **Noble resilience:** I loved my gentle father so much that I would do just about anything to get his praise, praise he always gave when I'd finished the job. I felt noble.
- **Character resilience:** I had promised Dad that I would do it, and I knew I just had to get it done to avoid guilt.
- **Ecological resilience:** I loved being outside and was grateful that I wasn't indoors having to clean my room.
- **Universal resilience:** With my Primary classes, I had been taught the power of prayer. I remember being very discouraged and I would offer simple prayers and plead to my Heavenly Father to help me get through a row.
- **Essential resilience:** When I knew the battle against the devil grass was looming, I knew I had to prepare for the day by getting enough sleep and a good breakfast to survive.
- **Intellectual resilience:** I kept trying to figure out a way to make the weeding easier—sometimes I would try watering the ground to make it softer. Sometimes I'd try a shovel, a hoe, or a pick.

The drives that were used to weed the devil grass are the same drives that you need to develop the grit and persistence to create a new identity. Ponder how these resilient drives will help you to act upon the creation of the new identity you formed in the previous section of this book. We can be as dogged and persistent as salmon in returning home to our Father in Heaven.

Maintaining the Luster of Your Treasury of Identities

You have an amazing treasury of identities that can help you to conquer today's challenges. You have had thousands of disruptions in your life, each with the opportunity of creating a new identity. When called to be a teacher, you became the identity of a teacher. When you were called to be a home or visiting teacher, you created a service-oriented identity to help other families. When you became a parent (if you are a parent), you became a whole bunch of identities: disciplinarian, nurturer, listener, protector—and the list goes on. In your home life, you assumed the identity as a cook, cleaner, and accountant. In your profession, you became several identities, such as hard worker, team player, and exemplar of the company image.

I repeat, you have a treasury of identities and you can use them to conquer life challenges. With some new experiences, you can go into your treasury and secure special combinations of identities to best conquer the life challenge. For example, as a parent, you may have to go back to your childhood to bring the playful identity and once again enjoy playing connecting with children on a playground. Think of times that you struggled with a task and finally figured out how to resolve the problem. Remember times when you may have struggled in school but resolved academic or social issues. Recall when you did well in school, in dancing, in athletics, in debate, or in any other activities that brought you joy.

It is important to keep the luster of your identities, particularly as it pertains to your experiences with memorable glory-rich experiences. In a journal or recording or other means to remember, document a time when you felt the Spirit in service. Remember times when you were reading a particular chapter or verse in the scriptures and the Spirit whispered a confirming testimony to you. Record your thoughts when you heard a spiritual message from the pulpit and it gave you a resonating or quickening moment. In the Church, you have learned the skills to perform a new calling. You have learned to teach. You learned to home teach or visiting teach.

In that magnificent treasury of experiences, you can recognize that each was a disruption and that you may have struggled, but upon reflection you see where you have conquered that challenge. These are positive recordings of life experiences where you were the conqueror and the attitudes, spirit, and grit helped you to be unbreakable. Remember that you have had more experiences where you were successful with a new identity than not. You can take courage as you reflect upon your treasury of identities.

Now, with each new life experience, you have the opportunity to formulate a new identity. You can reflect upon the sparkle of your treasury of identities and realize that you have the grit and persistence to thrive. With each new victory and new identity, you can continue to use glory of that experience throughout your life. With a new identity, you add to your arsenal of identity weapons for coping with life situations. Each time you reuse one of the identities, it becomes stronger with increased capacity.

I feel a little awkward sharing personal experiences, but they do illustrate the point I am trying to make. It is easy to remember the identity I had to develop to train as a high school and college athlete. I remember running hills, doing wind sprints, lifting weights, and working out until I almost dropped. The team had to become a "go until you drop" identity. Most of you can remember "go until you drop" mentality if you were on a mission, learning a musical instrument, or mastering subjects in school.

What was remarkable for me was that years after I finished my playing days in college, the feelings of "go until you drop" still come over me. In the introduction this book, I shared the experience of getting hit by the car and finding myself in a wheelchair with pins sticking out of my legs. I wanted to get better. After getting clearance from the physicians and counsel from physical therapists, I brought out the "go until you drop" identity that I had learned with the devil grass and in athletics.

> I didn't want people to feel sorry for me. I didn't see myself as a victim. I had had a marvelous experience

that changed me forever, and I just wanted to be physically functional again. I had caught a glimpse of my life purpose, and I wanted to have the thinking and communication skills so I could better fulfill that mission.

Suddenly it felt like my freshman year at college conditioning for the football team. The "go until I drop" identity consumed my soul as I worked as hard as I could on my rehabilitation. I had experienced a quickening confirmation that I would heal. I was determined to walk again. Many times, I would use my arms to lift myself off my wheelchair and try to take a step, but my legs were so weak they could not hold me. I would collapse in my chair—I had many moments of frustration and depression. I tried to hide my tears of discouragement from my family.

One day, my bishop came over to visit me to see how I was doing. He had visited regularly throughout this ordeal. He had seen me struggle for almost three months trying to get around in my wheelchair. On this visit, in our living room, I asked Bill to watch. With all the strength I could muster, I lifted myself from the wheelchair and took one step and then another without any support. I was shaky as a newborn calf, but I moved my legs. I took about six steps.

As I sat down again, tears streamed from my eyes. I could see tears on Bill's cheeks as well. As I have reflected upon that experience of taking my first steps, I compared them to treasury of other events in my life. I reflected how the "go until I drop" had resulted in celebrations from sports, academics and in my profession. None of these celebrations can touch the magnitude of joy and exuberance of taking those first precarious steps.

In our mortal experience, our mission and hope is to harvest as much glory as we can. Still mortality brings on more temptations and trials than we could have ever imagined. The next chapter will address the unbreakable path as well as the breakable path in our lives. It will address how to jump from a breakable path in life to an unbreakable path.

NOTES

1. James E. Faust, "The Power of Self-Mastery," *Ensign*, May 2000, 43.
2. Robert D. Hales, "To Act for Ourselves: The Gift and Blessings of Agency," *Ensign*, May 2006, 8.
3. Viktor E. Frankl, *Man's Search for Meaning*, trans. Ilse Lasch (Boston: Beacon Press, 2006), 66.
4. Ralph Waldo Emerson in *Teachings of the Presidents of the Church: Heber J. Grant*, 2002, 35.

9

Breakable or Unbreakable Saints

To become unbreakable, you need to continually keep your armor of God glimmering with the glory that is within you. Continually harvesting glory and remaining unbreakable is a challenge in today's world. The reality is that most of us have to fight off undesirable thoughts and habits. In fact, many of us struggle with questionable character-compromising habits. You may be suffering from thoughts and habits that, as hard as you try to be a resilient saint, you still find yourself thinking and doing things outside of your moral framework. When you think or do those things, you feel the light leave your soul and have feelings of guilt, discouragement, anxiety, or depression. You may forget your nobility and get too caught up in the temptation of this mortal world. We must live in the world and not of the world.

To this point in the book, we really haven't addressed those problems because the intent has been for you to discover, nurture, and act upon your strengths to find joy, happiness, and life progression. We have spent the first eight chapters in this book with the intent of helping you discover and nurture your innate strengths to be able to live an unbreakable path of glory. But life is far from blissful and problem-free for most of us. Sometimes your best planned actions do not result in fulfillment but rather in unhappiness and distress.

What is the real difference between the breakable path in life and the unbreakable path? So many characters in the scriptures and in Church history have been valiant but then became breakable. Starting at the beginning, Cain became angry and jealous and committed murder. David, blessed of God with power even as a boy to kill the great warrior Goliath, became breakable because of lust and adultery. Alma was heartbroken as he watched his blessed Nephite people become breakable because of pride and selfishness.

> And it came to pass in the eighth year of the reign of the judges, that the people of the church began to wax proud, because of their exceeding riches, and their fine silks, and their fine-twined linen, and because of their many flocks and herds, and their gold and their silver, and all manner of precious things, which they had obtained by their industry; and in all these things were they lifted up in the pride of their eyes, for they began to wear very costly apparel. (Alma 4:6)

Elder Dallin H. Oaks described how the three witnesses became broken but still clung to their testimonies.

> From a position of great influence and authority, all three witnesses fell, each in his own way. During 1837 there were intense financial and spiritual conflicts in Kirtland, Ohio. Martin Harris later said that he "lost

> confidence in Joseph Smith" and "his mind became darkened."[1]

Still, later in his life, Martin Harris was rebaptized in 1842 while living in Kirtland.

There are two general pathways in life that are riddled with emotions, decisions, and actions. One path is the path of acquiring glory with feelings of joy and the other is a path without glory that results in feelings of despair and guilt. There are obviously degrees of the amount of glory with one pathway as well as varying degrees of losing glory on the other. But for simplicity, we will consider two pathways. You are either progressing by harvesting glory or you are not. This chapter will help you dissect your thoughts and feelings along the unbreakable path. We will then examine the emotions and thoughts that follow the vulnerable and breakable pathway. Finally, we will address how we can conquer life challenges by jumping from the breakable path back onto the unbreakable path.

Cyclical Pattern of the Unbreakable Path with a Resilient Spirit

As alluded to throughout this book, you are on a foreordained path to harvest glory, which you have the agency to follow. Following a path strewn with glory suggests that you understand your resilient drives and are in harmony with your purpose and meaning of your noble resilience. Some people just go through each day to just get by. It sounds much like the exchange between the Cheshire cat and Alice Lewis Carroll's *Alice's Adventures in Wonderland*:

> "Would you tell me, please, which way I ought to go from here?"
>
> "That depends a good deal on where you want to get to," said the Cat.
>
> "I don't much care where—" said Alice.

> "Then it doesn't matter which way you go," said the Cat.
>
> "—so long as I get somewhere," Alice added as an explanation.
>
> "Oh, you're sure to do that," said the Cat, "if you only walk long enough."[2]

Too many of us are going along in life living only with routine and are lacking opportunities to progress. If you listen to the prompts that come from your glorious first estate sprit as well as the drives from your innate resilience, you will be on an unbreakable path to glory. In the world of philosophy, the path may be called a Path with Heart. Carlos Castaneda in his book *The Teachings of Don Juan* describes the path as follows:

> Look at every path closely and deliberately. . . . Then ask yourself, and yourself alone, one question. . . . Does this path have a heart? If it does, the path is good; if it doesn't, it is of no use.[3]

The unbreakable journey is the path with heart or as we are calling it in this book, a path of glory. Let's ponder the cyclical journey we make daily as a model. The model begins with your unbreakable core, which is step 1. Remember that your unbreakable resilient spirit is striving to communicate with your mind to harvest light, truth, and glory.

In step 1 you can see the resilient drives to harvest glory sending messages to your control center (the mind) to act upon your childlike, noble, and character resilience. You also recall that you are living in a sea of glory that comes from the intelligences and light from your ecological world as well as your spiritual world as shown in circle 2 on the model. It comes from the earth and nature as we have discussed. You are living, breathing, and receiving joy from the world around you if you are humble and receptive to it.

Your control center is shown as step 3. This is your mind, which tries to discern the prompts that come from your resilient spirit and the promptings that come from Holy Ghost. The challenge for your mind as the control center is to listen to the soft spiritual messages of glory that are sent to help you become aware, discern, and choose wise paths that will allow you to harvest glory and fulfill the yearnings of your spirit. The beginning of the model shows steps 1–3.

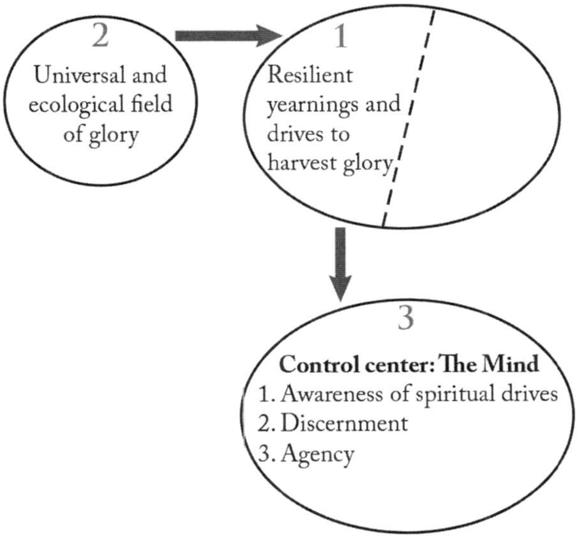

As we continue to build upon the model, you can see that your mind as the control center will hopefully choose to make wise choices in harmony with gospel ideals as shown in step 4.

Step 4 is the wise part of your control center. Step 5 is acting upon the wise spiritual prompts. It is taking leaps of faith to serve, learn, and make decisions based upon the glory based insights. You will feel fulfilled as indicated by the arrow that comes from the actions and leads back to the yearnings of your spirit (1). Fulfilling the prompts that come from the Spirit and acting upon them will allow you to again harvest a bit of glory as you return back to 1 by fulfilling the drives of the Spirit. This is the path of glory for the unbreakable saint.

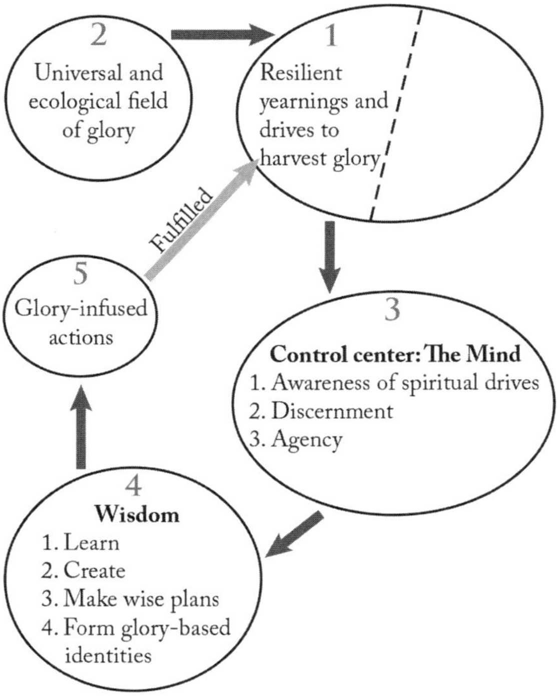

Your path of glory can begin each day as you think about your resilient spirit with its yearnings and drives to be childlike and noble and to live with character. You will want to think of your unbreakable path of glory in harmony with God and your ecosystem. Ponder some of the following questions that will help you have an unbreakable day with glory.

- How can I make my day more adventurous? (Childlike)
- How can I have more joy in my responsibilities today? (Childlike)
- How do I behave and think so that my armor of God will shine? (Character)
- How do I demonstrate honesty and integrity today? (Character)
- What acts of kindness can I do today? (Noble)
- How will I respond to my physical body's need for nutritious food, movement, and rest today? (Essential)
- What do I want to learn today? (Intellectual)

- How do I assure I make the right choices today? (Intellectual)
- What can I do to create an energizing or peaceful environment of glory at home, work, driving, or play? (Ecological)
- What can I do with listening to music, singing, or other sounds today to feel the Spirit? (Ecological)
- Where can I go today to pray to Heavenly Father to get strength to be unbreakable? (Ecological)
- What practices can I do today to connect with the glory in my world? (Universal)

Along the path with glory, we have thoughts and actions that optimally will result in a celebration in the Spirit (1) with an infusion of glory. A day harvesting glory is a day when you listen to your resilient yearnings and drives and take opportunities to fulfill them. When you face life challenges, you can find peace if you will use your resilient drives to help conquer life issues. You can then reflect back to your successes and feel the peace and joy of the path of glory.

Cyclical Pattern of the Breakable Path of Shadows

We try to begin each day on a cyclical path of glory. Sometimes our best efforts to fulfill the drives to fulfill our foreordination are thwarted through circumstances and choices at weak moments. Sometimes our plan for an unbreakable journey in a day is thwarted by temptations and problems. All of us sin to some degree or another and require the grace of the Atonement in the magnificent experience we call repentance. As hard as we strive to nurture our unbreakable spirits, still we sometimes find ourselves falling into the snares of the evil one. Often it happens because of a disappointment in ourselves or in someone else.

Sometimes our efforts are thwarted by others or by unexpected results from our plans of action. For example, we may try to do acts of kindness but be rejected by the receiver. We try to help someone else resist temptation, and instead that person turns on us in anger for intruding into their private world—an argument ensues. Sometimes we are so hungry to fulfill the drives of our innate resilience that mind chooses to violate the peace and rights of others. The bottom line, on the model, rather than an arrow of fulfillment going back to step 1 with glory, instead we find ourselves at step 6 being unfulfilled with a resulting void of glory (7). Adjacent to step 7, we see the feelings of not being fulfilled. We become struck with frustration, hurt, loss, guilt, fear, or confusion.

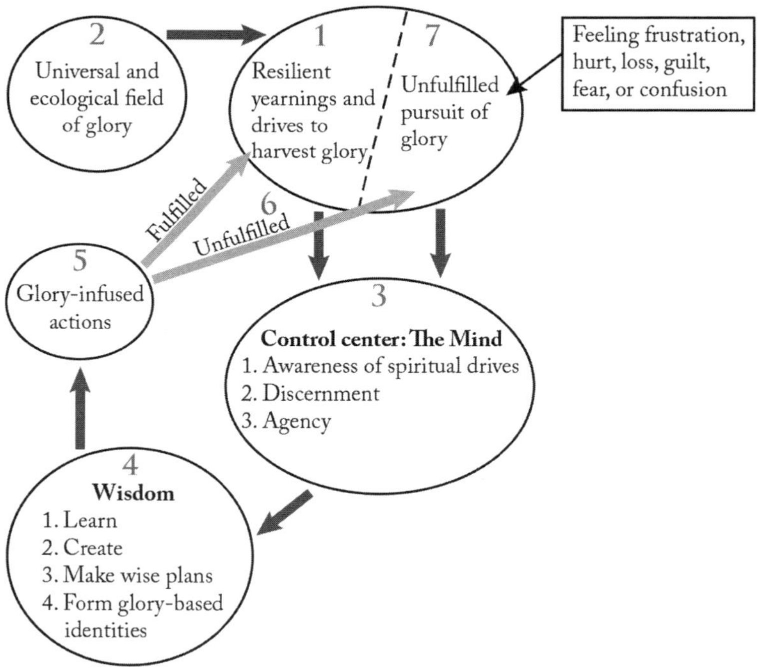

Actually, the mind (3) has an easier task of listening to your frustrated spirit because now the messages of hurt and loss are much louder. Now your control center exercises its agency. It (you) can choose to revisit your spiritual and resilient drives and determine whether there is still an opportunity to harvest glory by other actions. You choose the wise path (4). You create a new strategy to fulfill your resilient drives.

With one or more of the unfulfilled emotions coming to your mind, it opens the door for agency again. This time, your mind may resort to short-term unwise fixes for your unfulfilled spirit. You move to the mortal side of the cycle. We will call these shadows (9), which is what we call them in resiliency literature because the thoughts are devoid of light and truth. Shadows are the thoughts and cravings to do things that are glory draining or self-defeating. It is the mortal desire for quick pleasures that can potentially break you.

Your mind as the control center sometimes copes with unfulfilled yearnings in an unwise, short-term, and glory draining fashion. Shadows include the following descriptions:

- Shadows are secondary emotions, such as anger, jealously, or aggression.
- Shadows are the cravings to do something outside of the teaching of the gospel—what we call *sin*.
- Shadows are thoughts and feelings that lie outside of your moral and character code.

Shadow actions occur when you act upon the shadows (undesirable thoughts and cravings) and do what your character resilience does not want you to do. When you act upon the shadow actions, the aftermath will result in guilt, shame, and other unpleasant emotions, which divert you from the path of glory. You can see in the model that part of your mind is the shadow side (8). If we were thinking of a *Star Wars* movie, it would be the dark side of the Force. Acting upon the shadows or committing sin is shown as step 9 on the model.

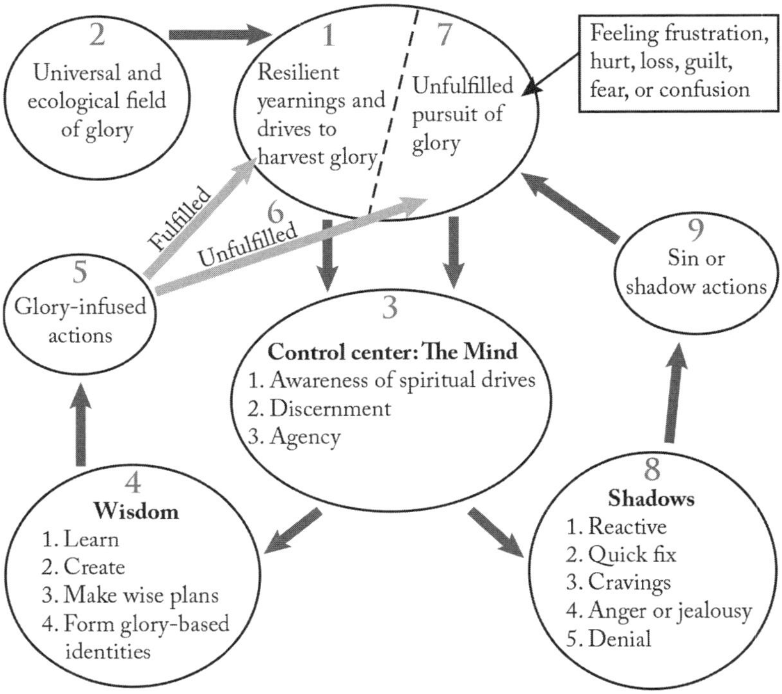

Some people become breakable when they experience the shadows in an argument with a loved one and get angry. Some try to find pleasure during difficult times and choose alcohol, pornography, or escaping into the entertainment world of movies and television. The thoughts of engaging in actions that are outside of your path of glory are the shadows. Acting upon the shadows are what can break you (9).

- smoking or chewing tobacco
- overusing alcohol
- uncontrolled gambling
- swearing
- overeating
- not getting enough sleep
- being addicted to electronic devices
- having other entertainment addictions (TV, sports)
- procrastinating and being lazy
- overusing prescription drugs

- being rude
- overspending
- using illicit drugs
- overusing caffeine
- watching pornography and having other undesirable sexual habits
- offending others (arguing, fighting, yelling, being overly critical)
- physically hurting other people or animals
- gossiping
- having body obsessions and eating disorders
- being dishonest or lying
- engaging in illegal activity (shoplifting, cheating on taxes)

We probably don't need a list of all the shadow actions because you are aware of them. But here is a list of several of mortality's frequent sins.

Shadow actions sabotage glory. We knew when we were born into this world that we would have opportunities for light and truth and also that we would encounter the shadows. In our lives, we witness and can read about the tug-of-war between opposing forces. For example, we read about:

- Good and evil
- Pleasure and pain
- Anima and animus
- Virtue and vice
- Yin and yang
- Positive and negative

You have essentially two choices when your shadows emerge. One choice is to do what your resilient spirit tells you to do, and the other is to yield to the shadow behaviors. Your resilient spirit wants to follow a path of glory. Your resilient spirit tells you to think and do things that will help you fulfill your childlike, noble, and universal resilient yearnings without compromising your character. The other choice is to follow the path of shadows, which is to do reactive actions that will eventually result in shame, guilt, and other unpleasant emotions.

The essence of the battle between the path of glory and the shadow path is conceptualized in this wonderful lesson from a Cherokee chief who was teaching his grandson about life.

> "A fight is going on inside me," he said to the boy. "It is a terrible fight, and it is between two wolves. One is evil—he is anger, envy, sorrow, regret, greed, arrogance, self-pity, guilt, resentment, inferiority, lies, false pride, superiority, and ego." He continued, "The other is good—he is joy, peace, love, hope, serenity, humility, kindness, benevolence, empathy, generosity, truth, compassion, and faith. This same fight is going on inside you—and inside every other person, too."
>
> The grandson thought about it for a minute and then asked his grandfather, "Which wolf will win?"
>
> The old Cherokee simply replied, "The one you feed."[4]

After sin or shadow actions, you find yourself back to an intensified step 7 or unfulfilled quest for glory. When time has passed, after you have engaged in shadow actions, you find yourself feeling guilty for your actions. You feel a loss of hope that you will ever be able to overcome your undesirable habit. These new unfulfilled feelings compound the initial unfulfilled yearnings, and now the pursuit of glory seems hopeless as your spirit aches.

You have returned to your soul's control center, the mind (3). Here you are even more aware of the crescendoing screams of your aching spirit and your unfulfilled spiritual quest for glory. The guilt for having engaged in the shadow action racks your soul. The scary thing about this cycle is that it can be never-ending if you do not make an effort to change. The more guilt you feel, the more you reach for the action that you are trying to eliminate. The cycle continues again and again. You drink alcohol excessively or use drugs, and then when the effect wears off, you go to the substances again to try to numb your guilt and other unpleasant emotions.

Now you know the two cycles. The path of glory when your mind with accompanying agency is wise and your actions are fulfilling. Wisdom tells you to continue on the path until you find a way to fulfill those yearnings. The other cycle is the path of shadows and sin, when you find yourself doing the things you regret and you become breakable.

DISSECTION OF THE SHADOW ACTION

At any point in time, when you are able to use your intellectual resilience to learn, discern, plan, and create a new identity, you can jump from the breakable path of shadows and jump to the path of glory. On the model, the flags indicate where you can make the jump from anywhere along the breakable path of shadows to your unbreakable soul's path of glory.

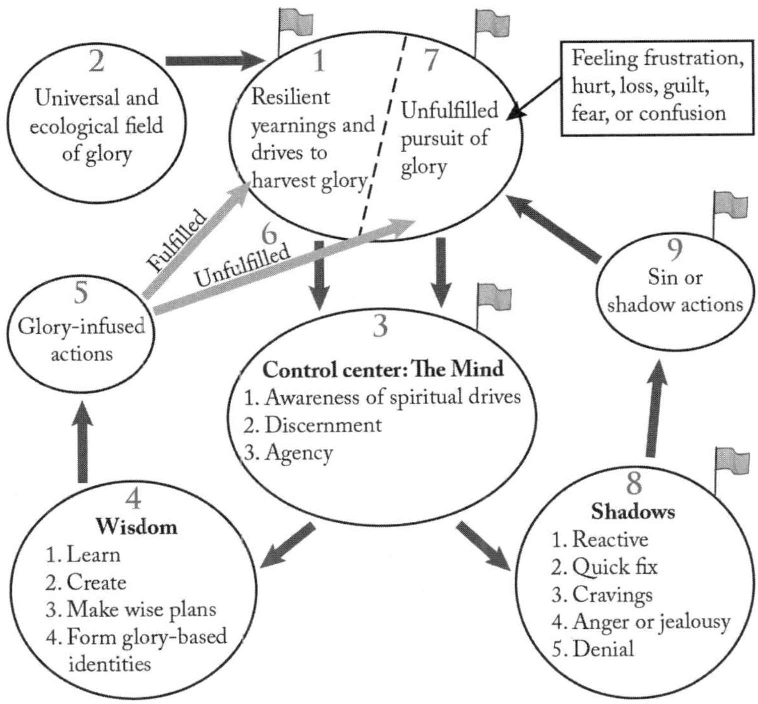

First, let's dissect the sin into its digressive parts that are weakening you and making you vulnerable to being broken.

- 9: The sin or shadow actions
- 8: The shadow: Secondary emotions, such as anger or jealousy, cravings for immediate pleasure, or craving to do things outside of your character resilience.
- 3: The mind as the control center: Your conscious mind senses the yearnings and promptings from both your glorified spirit and the darkened shadows.
- 7: The unfulfilled yearnings: When your resilient yearnings and drives are thwarted and frustrated, you will feel the hurt, loss, guilt, or fear.
- 1: Resilient drives to harvest glory and to be childlike, noble, to have character, to be enriched in your ecosystem, to be connected to the glory of God.

To understand the dissection of the devitalizing path of sin, let me provide a couple of examples of the dissection. We will first follow Jamie's story of ridding herself of an addiction.

> Jamie was a student at a university who was active in her student ward and held leadership positions in the Relief Society. During the summer just before school started, Jamie was on vacation with her family. While cliff jumping at a lake, she slipped and fell short of the deeper water in the lake. She landed in about seven feet of water, which was enough to buffer her fall, but her left foot landed on a rock, and she broke several bones in her lower leg.
>
> After several surgeries, she was in a cast and able to return to the university. In order to deal with the pain, especially at night, Jamie was given a prescription for pain relief—a narcotic, which was a potentially addicting substance if overused. It helped her sleep without pain. She found that the opiate seemed

to improve her mood in school and helped her cope with stress.

After a couple of weeks, her prescription expired, and on a follow-up visit to her physician, she asked her doctor for a refill, complaining of night pain. Reluctantly, the doctor provided the prescription. Jamie began to use the opiate more than once a day because she wanted the good feeling during the day as well. Her prescription again ran out, and when she requested more of the opiate from her physician, he refused.

Jamie went one night without the opiate, and she felt horrible. She knew that her father had some painkillers remaining from a surgery he had had. On a visit to her parents' home, she went into their bathroom and took the pills. Soon, she had used all her father's pills. She found a friend at her college that had ways to obtain more painkillers as well as other "feel-good" prescription drugs.

Over time, Jamie gradually found herself dependent upon a variety of painkillers, which began to affect her studies and social life. She also found that a significant part of her paycheck was going toward the purchase of pills.

Let's dissect Jamie's shadows.

- 9: The sin or shadow action: Taking pain pills well beyond the prescribed time and now beyond her control.
- 8: The shadow: Having a craving for pain pills she felt she needed to make it through a day.
- 3: The control center, the mind. As much as Jamie didn't want to take the pills, her mind could not think of any other way to feel good. The mind chose to pursue any way possible to find pills—taking the path of shadows rather than the path of glory.

- 7: The unfulfilled yearnings: Jamie became unhappy and dependent. The only way she thought she could fix the unhappiness and energy drain was with painkillers. Her guilt began to get worse to the point that she quit going to church.
- 1: The resilient yearnings of the soul: Jamie just wanted to be happy and enjoy life. She wanted to feel the spirit of the gospel and feel clean when taking the sacrament. She wished she had the strength to return to the path of glory.

I'll add a couple of other dissections, unrelated to the story, to assure that you can see the nature of each sin or shadow action. It is important to understand dissection in order to conquer life's challenges with a resilient spirit. (We'll continue Jamie's story later in the chapter.)

Dissecting Rebellion Against the Church

The shadow behavior would be becoming inactive and demeaning the Church and the leaders.

The shadow would be anger, jealously, envy, or frustration.

The mind determines that the best way to deal with the hurt would be to hurt back and meet with others to feel support in the efforts to devalue the Church. The aching of the heart could be from an embarrassing experience at a church meeting, loss of confidence in a church leader, or feeling inadequate to live the church standards.

The yearning of the heart is to feel connected, valued, worthy, and of worth.

Dissecting Backstabbing, Gossip, Bitterness, and Anger

The shadow behavior would be the actual backstabbing with accompanying bitter and angry comments.

The shadow would be anger, jealously, envy, or frustration.

The mind determines that the best way to deal with the hurt would be to hurt back.

The aching of the heart could be the frustration from feeling a loss of control, feeling devalued, or being disliked by others.

The yearning of the heart is to feel valued and of worth.

Dissecting Overeating (attempts to medicate the aching heart)

The shadow behavior is overeating.

The shadow is your mind craving food to medicate the aching of the heart through the pleasure of food. This may be conscious or more likely subconscious thinking.

The mind knows that food gives you a quick-fix pleasure rush.

The aching of the heart can come from any source of sadness or disappointment of unfulfilled yearnings. You may be trying to fix the guilt for stepping outside of your character code, hurt from a loved one, loss of control, or a number of other reasons.

The yearning of the heart is to feel peace for living within your moral framework, feeling control in an area other than food, or feeling loved by those we love. As far as overeating, it also wants to listen to your essential resilient drives to eat intuitively.

Try dissecting your own sins or shadow actions. Proceed to dissect it into its component parts and describe the parts of the shadow actions below.

The Shadow Action

____

____

____

____

____

Your Shadow

Your Conscious Mind

Your Aching Heart (Unfulfilled Yearnings)

Your Resilient Yearnings

____

____

____

____

____

____

____

____

TRIAL OF THE SHADOWS AND THE SHADOW ACTIONS

The snares of Satan are progressive and lead us into temptation and vulnerability one step at a time. If we respond to the allurement of the shadows, we can become a breakable saint. If we were in a courtroom, each of the characters along the path of shadows would contribute to the sin. At the same time, most of the characters can contribute to becoming an unbreakable saints. Let's put these characters on trial and see what sentences might be as they are handed down from the judge.

- **The Sin or Shadow Action (9):** Without consideration of any other factors, the shadow action has committed a violation of the commands and moral conduct. The key question is how you feel after time has passed about the action. Your glorified spirit testifies that there is no glory when the sin is committed. Since the focus is only on the sin, then the judge rules that the character of the shadow action is guilty. If it is guilty, then the sentence is elimination. We'll talk about how the elimination occurs after we consider the guilt or innocence of the other characters.

- **The Shadow (8):** Your cravings and secondary emotions did not actually commit the shadow actions. You craved substances outside of the Word of Wisdom. Your mortal passions were prompting you to transgress but still these were thoughts and cravings. The shadows of anger, jealously, and envy, still did not act but were precursors to action. The judge considers that even though the acts were not committed, still the shadow actions never would have been committed if it had not been for the shadows. The judge will rule that the shadow is an accomplice to the sin. The sentence will be to rehabilitation and probation.
- **The Control Center or Conscious Mind (3):** Your mind, as the control center, has the mortal agency to choose a path wisdom and glory (4) or to choose the path of shadows without light (8). In the process of dissecting the shadow actions, we can see that the mind according to the judge is also an accomplice. The sentence is mandatory training for the mind to learn to study things out, consider whether the actions will result in glory, and to control the cravings of the shadows.
- **The Unfulfilled Yearnings (7):** There is no guilt in the primary emotions of feeling hurt, loss, or fear. These emotions are, as indicated with the red flag, warnings that resilient drives to acquire glory are not being met. The mechanism to feel these stronger emotions allow the mind to listen more closely. These emotions are natural and normal and will be considered innocent. Their job is simple: to warn the mind that drives for glory are not being met.
- **The Resilient Yearnings of the Soul to Harvest Glory (1):** What can I say? The previous chapters have all focused on nurturing and responding to your resilient glorified spirit. Your soul is constantly sending message as to how to harvest glory through your resilient drives. Obviously, the judge declares the resilient yearnings to harvest glory as innocent. The sentence is to continue growing and guiding

in ways that will help to accomplish your mission and ordination on earth. It is to yearn to do things that will magnify your soul.

Carrying Out the Sentences

We are a society rich with ceremony; we wear caps and gowns at graduations and put on rings at weddings. We have enlightening ceremonies in sacrament meetings, in the temple, and when we are set apart in callings. Some of us use the ceremony of confessing to a bishop. Some post quotes from general authorities or pictures of the temple or the Savior as reminders to blaze a trail of new thoughts and behaviors. You can also create ceremonies to carry out the sentences for each of the characters involved with the shadow actions.

Your Resilient Drives to Harvest Glory (Your glorified spirit)

Based upon the trial, your yearnings to follow a path of glory are innocent and encouraged. You need the energy, motivation, and guidance from within your treasury of glory. You need your resilient drives to conquer your shadows and shadow actions. You are also encouraged to pursue activities that will strengthen moments when the infusions of glory can be felt. The more glory you find through serving others, reading scriptures, and praying, the more strength you will have to be unbreakable.

Unfulfilled Pursuit of Glory

In the trial, you determined that the unfulfilled yearnings and drives are innocent. You will feel the aching heart as warning signs or red flags to take wise actions to find another way to fulfill the yearnings. Your wise mind values the aching heart. Your mind will be trained to listen carefully to the aching spirit with unfulfilled yearnings.

Carrying out the Sentence for the Shadow Action

We will need to skip past the mind (3) and shadow (8) for now because their sentencing is a little more challenging. The shadow action or the sin is no longer allowed to be part of your life. Eliminating the behavior is important not only to be found worthy for gospel blessing but also to enjoy a guilt-free life. The energy you have used struggling with the shadows and shadow actions can be diverted into progression and positive actions in fulfilling your dream.

It is wise to make the execution of the shadow action a significant event. I would encourage you to have some type of ceremony when you are ready. The ensuing ceremony is an example of one way to create a ceremony to eliminate your shadow action. In preparation, be sure you are ready by reflecting upon how you feel in the aftermath of doing the shadow action. Remember the guilt and emptiness of spirit that results because of what you thought or what you have done. This kind of ceremony is a leap of faith, as per the resiliency process model, into a disruption, but the joy of self-mastering and eliminating your undesirable behavior is worth the leap. You may or may not want to include a trusted friend or family member to witness the ceremony and support you. First find a safe location where you can burn a piece of paper in a fireplace or open field. Try the following:

1. **Pick a time:** Appoint a designated time when you feel prepared and can devote your full attention to the change.
2. **Ponder the aftermath:** Ponder your sensitivities about how you have felt after you have participated in the shadow action. Feel the lack of glory and spirit. Focus on the guilt, hurt, or shame you felt by violating your sense of right and wrong and in some cases your covenants. Build your determination from your resilient drives to eliminate the action.

3. **Write the sin on paper:** Begin the ceremony by writing all the things you hate about the behavior. Write about your lack of control, the time you waste, and the secrecy. Write about how you feel when glory leaves your soul. Write about glory bleeding when the desired qualities of goodness, integrity, and morality fade. Write about your guilt, despair, and discouragement. Write all the things you can about the evil that the thoughts or behaviors brought into your life. Keep the paper or print it (saving it on your computer will help you to review this document later if you need it). Note: Another option is to draw a picture of the shadow action that encompasses your feeling.

4. **Remember the Atonement:** On another piece of paper, write your feelings about the Atonement and how it can help you rid yourself of the sin. Ponder the third article of faith and write its meaning to you.

> We believe that through the Atonement of Christ, all mankind may be saved, by obedience to the laws and ordinances of the Gospel.

Spend significant time pondering the magnificence of the Atonement and repentance and support them with scriptures. Reading, pondering, praying, and writing about King Benjamin's speech about the Atonement can help us remember its power. Spending time writing about your thoughts of even one verse can help prepare you for the execution of your sin.

> I say unto you, if ye have come to a knowledge of the goodness of God, and his matchless power, and his wisdom, and his patience, and his long-suffering towards the children of men; and also, the Atonement which has been prepared from the foundation of the world, that thereby salvation might come to him that should put his trust in the Lord, and should be diligent in keeping his commandments, and continue in the faith even

unto the end of his life, I mean the life of the mortal body. (Mosiah 4:6)

5. **Confirm your readiness:** With one piece of paper with your written expressions of disgust in one hand and the glory of the Atonement in the other, you can be ready for the execution. With a paper in each hand, you can sense the path of glory in one and the path of shadows in the other. Read again about the revulsion and disgust of the path of shadows and feel the spirit that come from the path of glory through the Atonement.
6. **The Execution:** In the safe location where you can burn a piece of paper and when you are 100 percent ready to forsake the sin, lift the piece of paper in the air. The paper is the shadow action, and you are going to execute it by burning. In your imagination, you can imagine that the fire is the Atonement and the glory of Christ. Light the paper, and as it burns, feel the purging of the sin from your soul. Feel the shadow action go away. It is no longer part of you. You have executed that shadow identity.
7. **Reminders:** Continue the ceremony by gathering the ashes, if you can, and burying them or putting them in a container that will remind you of your commitment. This will allow you to grieve and remind yourself of your repentance.
8. **Grieve:** As with any death, you may want to feel the loss of never being able to do that action again. You may want to create a psychological anchor, such as a jar with the ashes or some other symbol as a reminder. Some wear CTR rings or wear other rings with certain stones that represent your repentance experience. You may want to find a picture or poem that represents the loss of that behavior and your commitment to be free of the shadow action. For some time, you have used the shadow action to medicate your aching heart wounds. The reality of not ever being able to resort to it again creates a great sense of loss. The shadow behavior created an identity that is no longer part of who

you are. Spend some time, maybe a few days, to seriously grieve the loss of your shadow behavior.

9. **Make amends:** If your shadow archetype has offended others, do all you can to make up for it. It may be that a lot of collateral damage was done, and time will be needed for forgiveness to take place. Take whatever time you need to feel remorse and also to make amends.

10. **The shadow action is gone.** It is no longer a coping mechanism. You will no longer be able to use the action to cope with life challenges.

Let's continue with Jamie's story.

> Jamie woke up on a Saturday morning the week before her university spring break. She had a week without needing to attend classes. She started to crave her painkillers, but she had already taken her last pill. Suddenly, Jamie let out a scream of disgust. Her mind started to spin, as it always had, to scheme about how she was going to secure more pills.
>
> Jamie had been attending a resiliency class at the university, where she had received instruction on eliminating shadow behaviors. She started to reflect upon the time she had wasted and her horrible dependence on the pills. Anger began to boil up inside her, and the disgust reached a fever pitch. She hit her pillow again and again. Exasperated, she resolved to execute her addiction to pills.
>
> Jamie had loved backpacking all her life, so she packed some food and her camping gear and went up to the Uinta Mountains. She went to a favorite spot in the mountains and pitched a tent.
>
> In the evening after she had cooked her meal, she was sitting around the campfire thinking about how she would survive without the pills and at the same time was aching for the relief the pills could provide.

> As she had planned, she grabbed the empty prescription bottle from her last round of painkillers.
>
> She saw the bottle as the enemy. She cursed the bottle for all the misery it had put her through. She pleaded with God and the Savior to help her overcome this habit. She wrote her feelings of disgust with the pills down in her little notebook. She wrote on the front and the back of several pages. She also wrote her tender feelings about the Atonement.
>
> With great ceremony and determination, Jamie took the plastic prescription bottle and stuffed the little sheets of paper into the bottle. She then forced a small stick into the plastic prescription bottle with the notes of disgust. Ceremoniously, she slowly and with great ceremony and prayer put the prescription bottle and the notes first over the coals as she pondered the execution of her addiction. She then moved the bottle over the flames which she viewed as the Atonement and while it melted and burned, she felt an assuring strength that she could shake the need for these prescriptions.
>
> She wept as she struggled all night long craving the medication. She also cried because she felt the Spirit helping her to resist.
>
> The next day she went on a vigorous hike in the mountains. Half of her vigor came from being angry at herself for being in this situation and the other half of the energy came from the Spirit and hope of being rid of the pills forever. She knew she would have to endure a couple of weeks of struggle, but she was determined.

Sentence for the Mind: Wisdom or Shadow

The sentence for your mind is probation. Your mind has the agency to follow the path of glory or the path of shadows.

Understanding the progression to shadow actions is important because now your mind can be aware of where you are on the path. Here are some key ways to prepare to stay on the path of wisdom or jump from the shadows back to wisdom. As you think of actions that leave you vulnerable to becoming breakable, try the following:

1. Continue to fortify and enrich the path of glory. Have as many glory-producing experiences that you can through reading the scriptures, attending the temple, and attending meetings, etc.

2. Use your mind to create a plan to know automatically what you will do when your resilient yearnings are unfulfilled. If you are feeling empty because you have not had a glory-enriching experience in the gospel and feel spiritually stale, have a plan to go to your treasury of written spiritual experiences. Read your favorite scripture or go to someone you can talk to that you respect and can help you. If you are feeling a need for something exciting or pleasurable, have a plan in place. Rather than letting the unfulfilled feelings begin to think about the shadow actions, go play at a park with children, play a sport with friends, or gather some family or friends and do some singing. Go to a good movie or watch an engaging comedy and laugh. Become sensitive to these unfulfilled feelings, and when you feel empty, hurt, loss, or unfulfilled, then you see the red flag and you know what to do to get past the unfulfillment of the resilient yearnings.

3. If you are in the shadows and are already feeling cravings for substances, the cravings for pornography, or other intense negative emotions, have another plan in place. If you are angry or jealous, your plan may be to walk away from the situation and get into nature or some other setting to ponder your spiritual core. If you are sitting down at a computer and are tempted to find some pornography, have a plan in place. Perhaps you call a family member or someone in the

ward to see about their wellbeing. After being distracted with a red flag action, then focus again on building your spiritual core.

4. If you act on the shadows and tell that lie, yell at that person, take that drug, watch that pornographic movie, or whatever your shadow is, then focus on the consequences. After the short-term shadow pleasure or reaction is completed and given time, the glory in you will send messages of guilt to your mind. You are back on point 7. Now the unfulfilled yearnings are sending even louder messages and the guilt is amplified. The temptation is to seek the quick-fix pleasure shadow actions again to ease the guilt. The cyclic pattern from the aching of an unfulfilled heart to the mind's shadows and to the shadow action with the return trip to the aching is the life that too many of our brothers and sisters are living. The smiling faces on Sunday, if they come, are covering challenging paths of shadows. The solution is the same as before. When your mind feels the guilt, it is time for a new plan. Perhaps it is time to bring in a trusted family member or friend to hold your hand as you jump from the shadow path to the path of glory. Depending upon the severity of the shadow actions, it may be time to confess to a bishop.

The intent of the path of glory or path of shadows model is to help you discern where you might be on the cycle. It helps to know where you are and then to plan an escape from the path of shadows.

Let's finish the story about Jamie.

> When Jamie returned from her days camping in the Uintas, she could still feel the cravings for the pills. During her experience in the mountains, she planned her life to avoid the prescriptions and focused on building her path with heart.
>
> In the mountains, she had connected with nature and felt its calming effect. In her mind, she planned

> to hike every day, even if it was just in the neighboring park, just so that she could enjoy the natural rush of endorphins that substituted for the pain pills.
>
> Her plan was to go home and create a pseudo-mountain retreat in her bedroom. She got plants and posters to symbolize the strength she received from nature. She walked and biked most days to experience her natural rush. Jamie drew pictures and reminders and put them on her walls to help reflect upon the joys of freedom from her pills.
>
> She began to tell her story to trusted family and friends, which helped her to be the drug-free identity she had imagined in the mountains. Jamie became more physically fit and more spiritual.
>
> Over time, the cravings lessened and lessened. But each time a minor craving would come, she felt the red flag rise up within her, and she would respond with exercising, meditating, praying, or visiting one of her trusted friends. The energy she had previously put into finding drugs she now used to study the gospel and to exercise and nurture friendships, resulting in her becoming more physically fit and being invited to many social events, thus increasing her unbreakable spirit.

Benefits from Opposing Forces

The law of nature is that in order to create wholeness, there need to be opposing forces. Humankind knew this from the beginning. After Adam and Eve were forced to leave the Garden of Eden, they were introduced to the world of opposing forces and realized that there was no progression in the world of only bliss. To progress, they needed to be cast into a world where they would know good and evil, pleasure and pain, virtue and vice.

In 2 Nephi 2:25, we learn that "Adam fell that men might be; and men are, that they might have joy." The fall of Adam and Even brought joy over time. In physics, it is the positive charge of a proton coupled with the negative charge of an electron that forms an atom. In psychology, it is the anima and the animus for wholeness. In Chinese medicine, it is the yin and the yang. Developmental theorists speak of the drive for independence but also of the yearning to find comfort and security of companionship. Opposing essential yearnings strengthen your body in cycles, such as alertness combined with sleep. Both are requisite for health. As we look at the year's seasons, we see winter as a time of dormancy, but with spring, we see a drive among plants to grow and blossom.

The vision of the plan of salvation is to come to earth and be challenged by the temptations of mortality and use the gifts of the spirit to overcome them. You may drift to the path of shadows, but repentance through the Atonement provides an infusion of glory to help you to progress. We all bend, but in the trough and depths of humility, but we can receive strength to leave the path void of light and return to the path of strength, light, and truth. It is like the Zen story of the samurai warrior.

> A big, tough samurai once went to see a little monk. "Monk," he barked, in a voice accustomed to instant obedience, "teach me about heaven and hell!"
>
> The monk looked up at this mighty warrior and replied with utter disdain, "Teach you about heaven and hell? I couldn't teach you about anything. You're dumb. You're dirty. You're a disgrace, an embarrassment to the samurai class. Get out of my sight. I can't stand you."
>
> The samurai got furious. He shook, all red in the face, speechless with rage. He pulled out his sword, preparing to slay the monk.
>
> Looking straight into the samurai's eyes, the monk said softly, "That's hell."

> The samurai froze. The compassion of this monk who had risked his life to show him hell! He put down his sword and fell to his knees filled with gratitude.
>
> The monk said softly, "And that's heaven."[5]

Humbling experiences learned by Jamie and by the samurai show the power of the softness of glory. One of the most glorifying experiences in your life is when you leave the path of shadows and return to the path of glory. The concluding chapter will focus on wisdom. You will learn to see the world through the eyes of glory.

Notes

1. Dallin H. Oaks, "The Witness: Martin Harris," *Ensign*, May 1999, 37.
2. Lewis Carroll, *Alice's Adventures in Wonderland*, Macmillan Classics edition (London: Macmillan, 2014), 79–80.
3. Carlos Castaneda, *The Teachings of Don Juan: A Yaqui Way of Knowledge* (Los Angeles: University of California Press, 1968), 76.
4. "Native American Legends," *First People—The Legends*, accessed March 31, 2017, http://www.firstpeople.us/FP-Html-Legends/TwoWolves-Cherokee.html.
5. Fred Kofman, *Conscious Business: How to Build Value through Values* (Boulder, CO: Sounds True, 2006), 27.

10

WISDOM OF THE UNBREAKABLE SAINT

A good representation of how we conquer life's challenges is reflected in the 1989 movie *Indiana Jones and the Last Crusade*. In the film, we watch Indiana Jones in a desperate situation try to help his father. The Holy Grail, which will heal his father, is on the other side of a vast chasm. The process of venturing is demonstrated perfectly in a scene where he took a leap of faith. First, Indiana Jones studies an ancient manuscript that demonstrates how to cross the chasm. He has to study it out in his mind and figure out what to do. He knows he must step out to what appears to be certain death because all he can see is a thousand-foot drop off. But his study lets him know that if he takes the leap of faith, he will be able to get to the other side of the chasm. With a resonating faith and sense of urgency, he steps out into the deep chasm, but as he begins to fall, he is supported by a camouflaged bridge that takes him to the Holy Grail.[1]

As we engage in our mortal experience, we too find ourselves seeking our Holy Grails, or what we have been referring to in this book as light, truth, and glory. Venturing into the mortal experience from a glorious pre-earth existence, we too were like Indiana Jones as he took his leap of faith into the unknown. Sometimes, as unbreakable saints conquering life challenges with a resilient spirit, we find ourselves in the same situation as Indiana Jones. Let's try to summarize our leap of faith experience into the resiliency model and the plan of salvation model.

We know that in life you will choose or be forced again and again to leave your state of homeostasis and experience disruptions. You know that you will have the agency to decide whether the challenge will break you or whether it is only an experience that will ready you to receive insights from the field of glory that is within you and all around you.

As you take leaps of faith, you have the opportunity to receive answers to prayers and guidance on the path of glory to know what to do and how to do it. You have learned to create a new identity to conquer the new life challenge and by so doing add the identity to your treasury of experiences.

Each challenge in your life gives you the agency to reach into the treasury of glorified identities and create a combination of conscious identities to help you conquer the life challenges. If it is a totally new experience with the potential of breaking you, then you have the opportunity to create a new identity. To create the new identity, you can reflect upon your treasury of innate resilient drives and feel their energy and motivation. You know to fortify your body with adequate sleep, eat well for energy, and be as physically fit as you can be. You can then move forward, having armed your new identity with confirmations of rightness and infusion of glory through resonating and quickening.

With your soul full of spirit and energy, you can venture and take that leap of faith into using the new identity to conquer the new life challenge. With the leap of faith, you are celebrating the confirming power of glory. The outcome of the entire plan of salvation or resiliency model is that after taking leaps of faith or being blindsided by life events, each experience provides an opportunity to acquire wisdom as shown in stage 7 of the model.

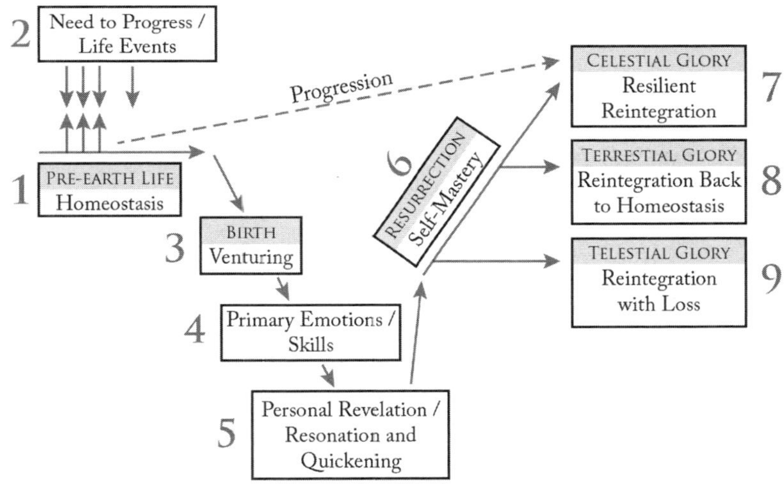

As we reflect again upon the resiliency model the optimal celestial choices embrace self-mastery and overcoming the shadows so that we find ourselves with more wisdom or in resiliency terms, we have resiliently reintegrated. Looking at box 8 on the model, we know that we could have had quickening personal revelations as to how to progress but didn't do it, so we reintegrated back to our comfort zones or homeostasis without increased light and truth. We have avoided or discarded the opportunity to harvest glory. If we found along the resilient journey that we reacted with shadows and shadow actions, then in all likelihood, we adapted to the experience with a loss of glory.

Wisdom is the accumulation of glory that we harvest one disruption at a time. Each time we conquer a life challenge we become stronger with a more resilient spirit. With each victory, we accumulate more glory and with the experiences more wisdom. Wisdom is one of the most important qualities to guide us through all of the challenges we hope to conquer.

> Seek not for riches but for wisdom, and behold, the mysteries of God shall be unfolded unto you, and then shall you be made rich. Behold, he that hath eternal life is rich. (D&C 6:7)

1. Wisdom is the product of experience after experience or resilient reintegration after resilient reintegration. It is the accumulation of glory, light, and truth after each new life challenge.

2. Wisdom is making choices that will allow you to harvest glory over time. We have to take leaps of faith, as per Indiana Jones, to harvest glory.

3. Wisdom is the magnificent series of revolutions as your human spirit assumes control of your entire soul and you become humbly submissive to the quiet, powerful, and true whisperings of the Spirit and our own yearnings for glory to progress.

4. Wisdom is evidenced by the manifestation of light and truth that have been harvested during the path of glory.

5. Wisdom is continually learning from life's disruptions. With each successful reintegration, you experience the infusion of confidence and faith.

As we think about the spiritual qualities of wisdom that result when we conquer life's challenges, some of the following come to mind:

1. **Appreciation and Gratitude:** You can look back at the challenges that you conquered and appreciate everything about the experience. You can appreciate and reflect upon the courage you had to face the challenges. You can be grateful to your Father in Heaven for providing a resonating and quickening moment. You can be grateful for the progression and the outcome of your resilient journey.

2. **Joy and Happiness:** Joy is the magnificent experience of receiving infusion of glory during times when we may be uncertain or afraid. It is the quickening of joy with the residual lingering of glory felt as happiness.

3. **Faith and Self-Efficacy:** As you reflect upon your leap of faith, you have garnered another identity—an identity that is willing to venture into challenges that can help you progress as long as it is confirmed by the Spirit. You did it once, you can do it again. Self-efficacy, the belief that you can accomplish things, increases experience upon experience.

4. **Peace:** Whether you are blindsided into a life event or you have taken a leap of faith, both experiences allow you to conquer life challenges. When you have resiliently reintegrated from a life challenge, your celebration of victory is interwoven with peace from the fabric of glory in your soul.

5. **Courage and Confidence:** Having experienced many resilient journeys, you can now reflect upon the initial fear you may have had but how through taking leaps of faith you surfaced more confident and with increased courage to conquer more life challenges.

Wisdom has been a prized gift of the Spirit from the beginning throughout the scriptures and in many cultures. Solomon was praised for his wisdom.

> And God gave Solomon wisdom and understanding exceeding much, and largeness of heart, even as the sand that is on the sea shore.
>
> And Solomon's wisdom excelled the wisdom of all the children of the east country, and all the wisdom of Egypt. (Kings 4:29–30)

We are encouraged to seek wisdom in Doctrine and Covenants 109:7.

> And as all have not faith, seek ye diligently and teach one another words of wisdom; yea, seek ye out of the best books words of wisdom, seek learning even by study and also by faith.

EYES OF GLORY

Unbreakable wisdom is to live your mortal life looking through the eyes of glory. Reading Doctrine and Covenants 88:11, we get a glimpse of the nature of eyes of glory.

> And if your eye be single to my glory, your whole bodies shall be filled with light, and there shall be no darkness in you; and that body which is filled with light comprehendeth all things. (D&C 88:67)

We know that being filled with light will help us to be unbreakable and able to conquer life challenges. We will understand and be quickened as we live our lives with the eyes of glory.

> And the light which shineth, which giveth you light, is through him who enlighteneth your eyes, which is the same light that quickeneth your understandings. (D&C 88:11)

As you face the challenges of mortality and walk a path of glory, seeing the world through eyes of glory, you will see life differently. With each life event, whether you have been blindsided or made poor choices or whether you have taken a leap of faith, you will live a happier life if you see it with the glory that comes from your resilient drives, the glory within you, and from the glory from the sea of glory in which you live. Wisdom then is to consider the resilient yearnings and drives that have been the focus of this book and to see your world with the eyes of glory.

Resilient Eyes of Glory

With an understanding of the resiliency process and how this life is a series of mini plans of salvation, you recognize that you will be disrupted thousands of times in your lifetime. To see the world through the eyes of glory is to see that with each disruption, there is an opportunity to harvest glory.

Sometimes when you face a difficult challenge, you know that you will struggle with feelings of hurt or anger or whatever, but you also know that if you humble yourself, the Spirit with its glory will lead you by the hand and give you glory and answers. You will celebrate the infusion of wisdom and then muster your grit and self-mastery and resiliently recover from the disruption. Your eyes of glory know that you will struggle but in struggling you can harvest glory. Your eyes of glory will be able to see the new identity that you have discovered to put in your arsenal of identity to conquer future life challenges. You will see all disruptions, no matter how minor or how major, as a journey to acquire new skills, identities, and glory. In your current life challenges, take a moment to see your current life challenge through the resilient eyes of glory and visualize how you will thrive through the resilient journey.

Childlike Eyes of Glory

Although some saints choose to bury their childlike nature, we know that your childlike qualities will help you conquer life challenges with a resilient spirit. Seeing your challenges with childlike eyes of glory helps you to become unbreakable.

- See your challenge as an adventure and muster the energy and motivation that comes with adventure.
- See the challenge as a chance to have fun or be playful. This may or may not be possible depending upon the situation, but do not assume difficult situations cannot involve fun. I remember walking by a waiting room in a hospital where a man's wife was in surgery. He was playing with his daughter to help with his challenge.
- See the humor in the challenge. You can think of the humorous stories you will tell about the difficult challenges when they are all over.
- See the opportunity to be creative in the challenge. Tackling challenges with creative new approaches brings bits of glory in the challenge.
- Face your challenge by remembering, seeing, and feeling the energy as a child.
- See the challenge as a chance to try something new and take calculated risks.

NOBLE EYES OF GLORY

Walking into church, in a grocery store, and any other time when you are with people, it is heartwarming to feel your yearnings be noble if you are looking through your noble eyes of glory. As you look at people, you can see in their faces a range of emotions and feelings. Being sensitive to your noble eyes, you will find opportunities to serve and help. By so doing their appreciation will infuse your soul with another bit of glory.

- See the challenge as an opportunity to become better and to learn.
- See the challenge as an opportunity to serve and help others.
- See the challenge as an opportunity for compassion and listening.
- See the challenge as an opportunity to believe in someone.

CHARACTER EYES OF GLORY

Remember that to preserve as much energy and spirit as you can to conquer life challenges you need to see your world through character eyes of glory. To enjoy the peace of a resilient spirit we should look through character eyes of glory.

- See the challenge through the eyes of honesty.
- See the challenge through the eyes of integrity.
- See the challenge through the eyes of honor.
- See the challenge through the eyes of loyalty.
- See the challenge through the eyes of fidelity.
- See the challenge through the eyes of fairness.

ECOLOGICAL EYES OF GLORY

As you look for the glory in the world around you, you can feel the peace that comes when looking at plants or trees or beautiful sunsets. You can feel the glory of God as you gaze upon snowcapped mountains or pristine lakes. As you walk through your life, use your eyes of glory to feel love when you see pictures of loved ones. Seeing the world through eyes of glory will help you appreciate the warmth and comfort of your home. You know that you can increase your energy and motivation to take on life challenges by feeling the infusion of glory come into your soul through selected music. You see the world of compassion and unconditional love as you find yourself around pets. See the world though ecological eyes of glory.

- See the life and energy in all living things.
- Feel the glory that come from natural things.
- Look for music, art, plants, people, and experiences that enliven your soul.

UNIVERSAL EYES OF GLORY

From chapter four on universal resilience, one of the most magnificent experiences that we can have is to see the world through the eyes of glory as we imagine and feel the intelligences and light from the presence of God all around us. Remember that you are walking, living, and breathing in a sea of glory that is within you and all around you—you can bathe yourself in that illuminating glory that will assure that you are unbreakable and able to conquer life challenges. Resilient spirits are those that harvest the glory in their worlds and harness the amazing love, wisdom, truth, light, guidance, and power that conquers life challenges.

- See the challenge through the eyes of your glorious spirit from the first estate and the magnificent sea of light, truth, and intelligences in your world now.
- As you strive to conquer life challenges with a resilient spirit, you can see through your eyes of glory, the comforting guidance and strength as the spirit embraces you soul.
- You can see your challenges being conquered with the glory that comes from the Father and the Savior.

ESSENTIAL EYES OF GLORY

Remember that the fabric of your physical body is glory. The wisdom of the glory will tell you when to move, what to eat, and when to sleep. As you look through the eyes of the fabric of glory in your body, you will do those things that will help to optimize your physical energy.

- See the challenge through the eyes of the amazingly perceptive body. What is the voice and wisdom of the body saying?
- See the challenge as an opportunity to improve fitness, energy, vitality, and overall health.

Intellectual Eyes of Glory

From the previous chapter, the mind becomes your control center and has the agency to look through the eyes of glory or the eyes of shadows. As you journey through your mortal existence, seeing the world through the eyes or path of glory is requisite to your personal progression.

- See the challenge through the eyes of either following the path of glory or the path of shadows.
- See the challenge as an opportunity and engage in brainstorming, increased creativity, and making decisions along the path of glory.
- See the challenge as an opportunity to increase in knowledge and faith.

Wisdom then is to see the world through the eyes of glory. Living resiliently is to see the world with eyes of glory through your big story of life as well as the numerous stories of disruption and reintegration that occur throughout the day. Consider the story that embraces eyes of glory demonstrated one day on a back road in Texas.

> George, an exercise physiologist, and I were driving back from Houston and heading home to College Station after a long day of presenting stress-management seminars at an accounting firm. We always loved to take the back roads in Texas because the country was so beautiful.
>
> We jumped off the freeway and were heading on this back road when we came to a few cars that were waiting for a truck to recover its load. We were about the fourth car to get there, and we debated whether to turn around or to wait. We opted to wait.
>
> It appeared that the truck had jackknifed. The trailer had been loaded with telephone poles and several of the poles had fallen off. The driver had a

forklift that had been strapped to the back of the trailer, and he was in the process of lifting the poles onto the now-straightened truck and trailer, one pole at a time. His truck and poles totally blocked the two-lane road.

George and I were only about ten miles away from being home, so we were a little frustrated. We noticed that some of the other people waiting for the driver to finish loading his telephone poles were also upset. They had gotten out of their cars and began to stand or walk around mumbling to each other because of the wait.

As George and I got out of the car, we could hear conversations about the truck driver and his marginal IQ. While all this stress was being put on this poor truck driver, I joked with George and said, "Which of those stress-management strategies we just taught for the accountants would work for this guy?"

Then I noticed that the driver on the forklift was smiling and giggling. I said, "George, look at that guy—he's smiling and laughing. Either he's fruit loops or we need to find out how he's dealing with this stress in such a positive way. When we find that out, we'll bottle it and sell it!"

George and I got closer. Between the driver's knees, sitting on the chair of the forklift, was a five- or six-year-old boy. The driver and his boy were playing tractor—on our time! The little boy and dad had their hands on the lever and were having a great time loading the telephone poles one at a time. They were totally oblivious to the grumblings of those who waited.

Here was the great principle: you see disruptions as opportunities to love, play, and have adventures. When you focus on your strengths as opposed to the external stressors (the irate observers), the problems

> have a tendency to go away. This driver saw the world through the eyes of glory and his disruption an opportunity for childlike infusions of glory.

Conquering Challenges with a Resilient Spirit

The resilient spirit will help you to conquer all of life challenges. Consider some of the following life challenges and remember from the chapters in this book how to conquer them:

1. When you are afraid, the infusions of glory will help you to channel the energy of fear into the power of courage. We spoke of venturing and turning fear into courage by loading the scales of balance to the "path with heart" side of the scale with resilient drives and reducing fears through understanding.
2. When encountering stressors, the infusion of glory will help you embrace those stressors as springboards for growth. You learned the resiliency process model and resiliency mapping in chapter 1.
3. When facing great adversity, the infusion of glory will help you find strength beyond your normal capacity to thrive. You have learned of the tremendous forces within you and in the world around you to guide and strengthen you to overcome that adversity.
4. When feeling confused at a time of important decision making, the infusion of glory will help you discern, choose, and gain confidence in your choice. You will remember that confusion is a precursor and sign of readiness to receive the answers through the experience of resonation and quickening.
5. When feeling down and discouraged, the infusion of glory will help you discover jewels of hope in the mire of depression. After experiencing all the resiliency concepts, you know the journey. You can almost celebrate frustration

because you know it is just for a moment and an opportunity to use readiness skills to resiliently reintegrate.

6. When you are feeling anxious, the infusion of glory will bring you calm and peace. Anxiety produces tremendous energy that you can potentially transform into courage with accompanying calm and peace.

7. When you are held captive by shadow actions, the infusion of glory will empower you with strength and control. Chapter 9 took you through the process of dissecting your shadow actions and described how you can access strength and control.

8. When you are angry, the infusion of glory will help your mind to stop, reflect, and return to the path with heart.

9. When faced with situations beyond your control, the infusion of glory will help you find peace and acceptance. With the light and truth from within you and around you, you can learn to find energy to conquer those things you can control and find peace and acceptance for things you cannot control.

10. When concerned about what is right, the infusion of glory will confirm your truth. The glory of truths revealed come through resonation and quickening and is the infusion of truth.

11. When tired, the infusion of glory will infuse you with increased capacity to think, perform, and do. With the blessing of receiving intelligences and truth by doing those things that are along your path with heart, you can celebrate renewed energy from your resilient drives and the glory around you.

12. When you need to create a turning point in your life, the infusion of glory will infuse your spirit and mind with insights to know which way to turn. You will know that the direction you will take will be within your character,

noble, and universal resilience. You will be able to discern between a path with heart and a path of shadows. You can be quickened to the right direction.

The Applied Theory of Everything

The infusion of glory is truly the applied theory of everything from a resiliency perspective. As you walk through life with its accompanying disruptions, you will be faced with choices. You will be faced with a need to feel increased energy, courage, patience, hope, and power to thrive though life challenges. You will need to feel self-worth and value. You will want to have fun and adventures. You will need to know what is right, fair, and honest. Every facet of your life will be enriched with childlike, noble, character, universal, ecological, essential, and intellectual resilient glory.

The means to make everything optimal in your life is through the magnificent infusion of the glory that will help you to know what to do, when to do it, and how to do it. To repeat from earlier, the applied theory of everything and all of the answers to everything are wrapped up in one scripture.

> Be thou humble; and the Lord thy God shall lead thee by the hand, and give thee answer to thy prayers. (D&C 112:10)

The purpose of life is to harvest glory in all of its sources. It is all about being led by the hand that comes in the form of resonation or in the form of quickening. The leading comes through the subtle vibrating guidance and knowing that you are on a path with a heart of resonation. It is the course-adjusting and course-informing jolt of quickening to give you testimony and alter the direction you need to take to optimize your life.

Write Your Conquering Story with You as the Unbreakable Saint

As you ponder these thoughts of your resilient drives of being childlike, noble, and live within character, how can your story evolve from now to the future? As you ponder walking through the world with the eyes of glory, how does your life story evolve?

This is not a quick exercise but one that you should write over time. Part of your story will be your own personal journey. The other part of your journey is to touch the lives of others. As you learn it, then you will want to live it. And after you live it, you will want to teach it.

It is my sincere hope that you will benefit and that, as you learn and experience the lessons of the infusion of glory and resilience, you will be moved to share what you have learned with others. Lasting change occurs when you become a role model or a teacher. When you teach a spouse, a child, or a friend, it forces you to remember, better understand, apply, and live the principles. Walking the path of glory will be noticed by others, and they will want to be part of your vision and wisdom. Write a few thoughts to trigger your mind as you write your story.

Portions of this book have been about writing my own story. I have reflected often upon the spiritual gift I received when I was hit by the car and was forced into the coma. On the journey to write my story, let me close this book with my reflection of my life-changing accident.

> As I reflected upon what I had learned, perhaps the biggest change was how I saw the world. Walking across campus, I would look at students and faculty and sense their energy and countenance. I knew they all had stories—they were in the midst of a story as I passed them on the walkways. I looked at animals differently. I would look into dogs' eyes to try and feel their spirit—they became friends.
>
> I had learned that I was walking, living, and breathing in a magnificent sea of energy, wisdom, courage, hope, and power—a sea of spirit. My academic and professional passion had now become to study resilience and resiliency, which is really applying gospel principles to academia. I created graduate and undergraduate classes on resilience to try to touch the lives of those wonderful souls I am privileged to teach. It has been a joy to travel to places

> around the world and try to touch lives by speaking at professional meetings. I have learned so much in this rehabilitation process. The experiences of the coma, in the hospital, and rehabilitation became the foundation of a whole new life and purpose for me.

My sincere wish is that all of us can witness and experience the awe and wonder of the world of light and truth as we see the world through eyes of glory. The spirit world is real. The sea of glory in which we live is real. Through the disruptions you experience on a regular basis, you will be able access the treasury of memories and identities that are rich with glory and will enable you to conquer life challenges with your resilient and unbreakable spirit.

NOTE

1. *Indiana Jones and the Last Crusade*, directed by Steven Spielberg (Hollywood: Paramount Pictures, 1989), DVD.

Personal Notes

PERSONAL NOTES

References

Ballard, M. Russell. "Purity Precedes Power." *Ensign*, November 1990.

Bateman, Merrill J., and Marilyn S. Bateman. "Mortality and Our Eternal Journey." Brigham Young University devotional. January 14, 2003. speeches.byu.edu.

Carroll, Lewis. *Alice's Adventures in Wonderland*. Macmillan Classics edition. London: Macmillan, 2014.

Castaneda, Carlos. *The Teachings of Don Juan: A Yaqui Way of Knowledge*. Los Angeles: University of California Press, 1968.

Chardin, Jean. *Voyages en Perse et autres lieux de l'Orient* [Journeys in Persia and other places of the East]. Amsterdam: chez Jean Louis de Lorme, 1711.

Conwell, Russell H. "Acres of Diamonds." Temple University. Accessed March 28, 2017. https://www.temple.edu/about/history-and-traditions/acres-diamonds.

Csíkszentmihályi, Mihaly. *Finding Flow: The Psychology of Engagement with Everyday Life*. New York: Basic Books, 1997.

Dickens, Charles. *A Tale of Two Cities*. London: Chapman & Hall, 1859.

Emerson, Ralph Waldo. *Lectures and Biographical Sketches*. Cambridge: The Riverside Press, 1886.

———. In *Teachings of the Presidents of the Church: Heber J. Grant*. 2002.

Faust, James E. "The Power of Self-Mastery." *Ensign*, May 2000.

Feynman, Richard P. *Six Easy Pieces: The Fundamentals of Physics Explained*. Harmondsworth: Penguin, 1998.

Frankl, Viktor E. *Man's Search for Meaning*. Translated by Ilse Lasch. Boston: Beacon Press, 2006.

Fulghum, Robert. *All I Really Need to Know I Learned in Kindergarten: Uncommon Thoughts on Common Things*. New York: Villard Books, 1990.

Gandhi, Mahatma. *Teachings of Mahatma Gandhi*. Lahore: Indian Printing Works, 1947.

Greene, Brian. *The Elegant Universe*. Directed by Joseph McMaster, David Hickman, and Julia Cort. Aired September 28, 2003. Boston: NOVA, 2003. http://www.pbs.org/wgbh/nova/physics/elegant-universe.html.

———. *The Elegant Universe: Superstrings, Hidden Dimensions, and the Quest for the Ultimate Theory*. New York: W. W. Norton, 1999.

Hales, Robert D. "To Act for Ourselves: The Gift and Blessings of Agency." *Ensign*, May 2006.

Indiana Jones and the Last Crusade. Directed by Steven Spielberg. Hollywood: Paramount Pictures, 1989. DVD.

Jung, Carl. "The Concept of the Collective Unconscious." Vol. 9 of *The Collected Works of C. G. Jung: The Archetypes and the Collective Unconscious.* Princeton: Princeton University Press, 1968.

Kimmerer, Robin Wall. *Braiding Sweetgrass: Indigenous Wisdom, Scientific Knowledge, and the Teachings of Plants.* Minneapolis: Milkweed Editions, 2013.

Kofman, Fred. *Conscious Business: How to Build Value through Values.* Boulder, CO: Sounds True, 2006.

Lao Tzu. *Tao Te Ching: The New Translation.* Translated by Jonathan Star. New York: Penguin, 2008.

———. In Joseph A. Magno, *The Spiritual Philosophy of the Tao Te Ching.* Chicago: Pendragon Publishing, 2005.

The Lion King. Directed by Roger Allers and Rob Minkoff. Burbank, CA: Buena Vista Pictures, 1994. DVD.

Maxwell, Neal A. "Lest Ye Be Wearied and Faint in Your Minds." *Ensign*, May 1991.

McTaggart, Lynne. *The Field: The Quest for the Secret Force of the Universe.* New York: Harper Perennial, 2008.

"Native American Legends." *First People—The Legends.* Accessed March 31, 2017. http://www.firstpeople.us/FP-Html-Legends/TwoWolves-Cherokee.html.

Nelson, Russell M. "The Magnificence of Man." *New Era*, October 1987.

———. "We are Children of God." *Ensign*, November 1998.

"O My Father." *Hymns*, no. 292.

Oaks, Dallin H. "Revelation." Brigham Young University devotional. September 29, 1981. speeches.byu.edu.

———. "The Witness: Martin Harris." *Ensign*, May 1999.

Packer, Boyd K. "Personal Revelation: The Gift, the Test, and the Promise." *Ensign*, November 1994.

Palmer, William. In David O. McKay. "Pioneer Women." *Relief Society Magazine*, January 1948.

Richardson, Glenn E. "The Metatheory of Resilience and Resiliency." *Journal of Clinical Psychology* 58, no. 3 (March 2002): 307–21, doi: 10.1002/jclp.10020.

———. *Proactive and Applied Resilience: The Sixteen Experiences.* Bloomington, IN: iUniverse, forthcoming.

Seligman, Martin. "The New Era of Positive Psychology." Presentation at TED2004 conference. Monterey, California. February 25–28, 2004.

Smith, Joseph. *Teachings of the Presidents of the Church: Joseph Smith.* 2011.

Smith, Joseph F. *Gospel Doctrine.* Salt Lake City: Deseret Book, 1977.

Sternberg, Esther M. *Healing Spaces: The Science of Place and Well-Being.* Cambridge: Harvard University Press, 2009.

Tallmadge, Benjamin. *Memoir of Colonel Benjamin Tallmadge.* New York: Thomas Holman, 1858.

"A Thought for Every Day," *Milady Beautiful* 8, no. 4. January 1919.

Uchtdorf, Dieter F. "The Love of God." *Ensign*, November 2009.

———. "Your Wonderful Journey Home." *Ensign*, May 2013.

Washington, George. *George Washington to the Connecticut Legislature, October 17, 1789.* Letter. From Library of Congress, *The George Washington Papers.*

Williamson, Marianne. *A Return to Love: Reflections on the Principles of "A Course in Miracles."* New York: HarperCollins, 1992.

ABOUT THE AUTHOR

Glenn E. Richardson received his bachelor's degree in zoology from Southern Utah University, his master's degree in exercise physiology from Utah State University, and his PhD in health science from the University of Utah. He has held academic appointments at the University of Kentucky and Texas A&M University and is currently a full professor at the University of Utah. He has authored seven academic books and published dozens of papers in scholarly journals. He has provided trainings, speeches, and workshops to over seven hundred audiences in most US states and in several countries (Australia, the Bahamas, Canada, Mexico, and Brazil). His most cited seminal article is entitled "The Metatheory of

Resilience and Resiliency," which was published in the *Journal of Clinical Psychology*. His most recent book is entitled *Proactive and Applied Resilience: The Sixteen Experiences* and will be published about the same time as *Unbreakable Saints*. Glenn has been teaching graduate and undergraduate integrative health and resiliency classes at the University of Utah continuously since his first resiliency article was published in 1990.

Glenn has been active in the Church his entire life. He is married to Kathryn Maye Richardson, and together they have six children. His nickname away from the university is "Buzz." Buzz served a mission in Brazil. Most of Buzz's Church service has been with the youth. He has been the force behind multiple youth conferences and spoken at numerous youth, young adult, and single adult firesides. He has been a scoutmaster, explorer leader, and stake Young Men president as well as serving in bishoprics and high councils in Kentucky, Texas, and Utah. He has presented at BYU education week.

Buzz's greatest joy is to laugh, play, and joke with his family. Buzz attributes his coming out of shyness to his playing sports in high school and college. Buzz loves being in the outdoors, with animals, and being in nature. He enjoys pondering life's purpose and meaning as well as the "so what" of gospel teachings. Glenn loves the Savior.

Scan to visit

www.glennrichardsonbooks.com